MAX NEWNHAM

Funding Your Retirement

A Survival Guide

Wrightbooks

First published 2011 by Wrightbooks
an imprint of John Wiley & Sons Australia, Ltd
42 McDougall Street, Milton Qld 4064

Office also in Melbourne

Typeset in Granjon 12/15 pt

© Max Newnham 2011

The moral rights of the author have been asserted

National Library of Australia Cataloguing-in-Publication data:

Author:	Newnham, Max.
Title:	Funding your retirement: a survival guide /Max Newnham.
ISBN:	9780730375081 (pbk.)
Notes:	Includes index.
Subjects:	Retirees — Australia — Finance, Personal.
	Retirement — Economic aspects — Australia.
	Retirement income — Australia.
	Retirement — Australia — Planning.
Dewey number:	332.0240140994

Cover images: © Stiggy Photo, 2011; © Danny E Hooks, 2011; © STILLFX, 2011; © Robyn MacKenzie, 2011; © Iakov Kalinin, 2011. All images used under license from Shutterstock.com.

Table 3.4 and tables 17, 18, 19, 20, 21, 22 in appendix: reproduced with permission from Centrelink. Rates are current as of March 2011. Readers need to refer to <www.centrelink. gov.au> for up-to-date Centrelink information.

'The 10 worst stock market crashes on the New York Stock Exchange since 1900', pages 178–179. Source: <www.frankrank.com>. Used with permission.

Tables 3.1, 3.2, 4.1, 4.2, 4.3, 6.3 and tables 3, 4, 5, 6, 7, 8, 13 in appendix: © Australian Taxation Office. The ATO material included in this publication was current at the time of publishing. Readers should refer to <www.ato.gov.au> for up-to-date ATO information.

Printed in Australia by Ligare Book Printer

10 9 8 7 6 5 4 3 2 1

Disclaimer

Contents

Also by Max Newnham

Tax for Small Business: A Survival Guide
Self Managed Superannuation Funds:
A Survival Guide

About the author

Max Newnham is a chartered accountant who has been working in public accounting since 1974. He is a partner in the firm TaxBiz Australia, which has two offices in the outer eastern suburbs of Melbourne and looks after clients from all around Australia.

Like many chartered accountants, Max started his professional life in auditing, moved into insolvency, and then found his niche in looking after the tax, accounting and financial affairs of small business owners and individuals.

Worried about the quality of financial advice his clients were receiving from commission-driven financial planners, Max became a certified financial planner (CFP) and gained the designation of Chartered Accountant—Financial Planning Specialist. He is also a specialist adviser on self managed super funds (SMSFs) to the Self-Managed Super Fund Professionals' Association of Australia.

During the mid 1980s, when Australia had, in Max's opinion, the world's greatest treasurer, Max mounted a media campaign against the Australian Taxation Office (ATO), which was disadvantaging low-income earners who had been made redundant. This campaign led to the Hawke government issuing legislation to force the ATO to stop overtaxing lump sum termination payments, and was also the start of Max's writing career. The firm he was working with at the time, recognising his interest in tax issues, asked Max to write tax articles that they issued as press releases. When he started his own firm in 1989, he became a columnist for the weekly *Money* section in the Melbourne's *The Age* and *The Sydney Morning Herald*. The topics Max covered in these articles increased in range to include not only tax, but also small-business issues, superannuation and investing.

At the same time Max attended his first federal budget as part of *The Age's* budget coverage team, preparing tables and other analysis related to budget and tax issues. Since 1989 he has covered every federal budget except for one.

The articles he loves writing most come from interviewing people, ranging from Lindsay Fox to The Waifs, about what it takes to be successful in business. A collection of these stories formed his third book, published as *Great Aussie Success Stories*. Keeping up with these modern electronic times, Max now also writes weekly columns for the online version of Fairfax publications on small business and investing issues.

Max's first book dealt with the introduction of the goods and services tax (GST), and the second with the introduction of the new superannuation system. He has written three books for Wiley: *Tax for Small Business*, *Self Managed Superannuation Funds*, and now this one, which are all written as survival guides.

Max lives in an outer eastern suburb of Melbourne in the beautiful Dandenong Ranges. He and his wife are fast becoming empty-nesters (not before time) and are looking forward to a long and happy retirement in the not too distant future. Their six children have all embarked on different careers and they have two grandchildren, an old dog, and a young puppy that keeps everyone on their toes.

Acknowledgements

There are many people I need to thank for having helped through the gestation period and the birth of this book. First of all, thanks to Kristen Hammond from Wiley, who alternated between being my mentor and chief whip cracker, liked my idea for this book and came up with its title and so its direction.

To Daniel Dutt, my right-hand man at TaxBiz financial services, a big thank you for proofreading the chapters relating to financial planning. My wife, Liz, deserves a medal for shouldering more than her fair share of the household duties while I wrote this book.

To all of the editors and subeditors I've worked with over the years in the Fairfax organisation, thank you for giving me the opportunity to fulfil a lifelong ambition to write — and even get paid for it. Thank you to Michael Wilkinson who talked me into writing my first book, and Steve Berry from Fairfax Publications for championing my next two books. Steve, you are sorely missed.

A last big thank you to Mr Wallace, my fifth form English teacher at Mitcham High, who failed me in his subject. This meant I repeated the year, got to do an extra year of accounting, and ended up in a class where the girls outnumbered the boys by five to one.

Introduction

This book is meant to be a practical guide for anyone interested in having a financially secure retirement. At times technical points must be discussed, but this book is designed to be a step-by-step guide to help people who want to help themselves.

It is not a get-rich-quick, or get-rich-slow, guide based on teaching the principles of borrowing against property and becoming a tycoon that way. It won't explain the mysteries of foreign exchange or derivative trading so you have some secret way of making money known only to the incredibly clever. And it won't tell you how you can apply the principles of some of history's greatest share investors and become as rich as Warren Buffett.

This is a book about having a balance in life and investing that takes the long-term view. It does not come from my having studied endless tomes about theoretical investing. Instead it comes from more than 50 years of personal investing and from almost 40 years of advising people about money and tax.

You will notice that the title of this book is not 'Saving for Your Retirement'. This is because there is a major difference between saving and investing. Saving is what most people do when they put money in bank accounts, jam jars or any other receptacle. It is squirrelling money away without a goal. Investing is about first deciding what you want to achieve, and then putting in place a plan to achieve those goals.

The problem with savings is that they get spent. This is because the savings build up and, when there isn't a purpose for them, they are spent on what often seems like a good idea at the time. It could be on the holiday you have always wanted, the plasma screen that you just had to have, or the whole new wardrobe you needed because you couldn't find a thing to wear.

The unfortunate truth about most people's financial life and retirement is that it is similar to an impulsive decision to travel. They walk out their front door, get in whatever vehicle is sitting in the driveway, and start driving. After a time, the length of which varies between people, they find themselves in a place called retirement and they have to make do with what they have.

Whenever I am going on a journey I like to decide where I'd like to end up first. I then work out the best way of getting there, and what I would like to see along the way. I calculate how much it will cost to get there, and what it is going to cost once I have arrived. Then I start to organise my travel plans and finances accordingly.

Planning for a comfortable retirement should be exactly the same. You first need to decide when you want to retire, what your lifestyle will be and how much income you will need to fund it. You then need to put in place the plans to help you reach your retirement destination.

I am writing this book with an old proverb in mind: 'If you give someone a fish, you feed them for a day. If you teach them how to fish, you feed them for life'. This book is all about teaching you how to take control of your financial life so you can enjoy a financially secure retirement.

My personal experience with investing started with my first job as a paperboy selling newspapers on cold winter mornings. I was earning roughly 20 shillings a week. That clearly makes me a baby boomer, as this was before dollars and cents and it was not long after Melbourne first got black and white TV. I had the choice of either spending this newfound wealth or achieving something with it. I soon worked out that I wanted to take up photography and have some money to spend over my Christmas holidays.

Once my goals were set, I worked out how much the camera would cost and what I wanted to spend over the holidays. I then opened a bank account and deposited the part of my weekly wage needed to achieve my goals. By the time Christmas came I had my camera and enough money to enjoy my holidays.

Another important part of funding your retirement is managing both your investments and your expenses to ensure your funds last as long as they need to. Although this appears to be an obvious step it is one often missed. It is all about organising your investments so they produce enough income, and controlling your expenses so they don't exceed your income so you are forced to sell investments.

This concept of making your funds last — and at the risk of confirming in your mind that I was born a boring accountant — became obvious to me before starting the six-week summer holidays: I realised if I wanted my money to last, I needed to work out how much I could spend each day.

Great Moments in Accountancy

Source: <www.CartoonStock.com>.

As a Gemini, this appealed to the logical half of my brain, which I guess is why I ended up in accounting, a profession based on logic that has a balance to it. For every debit there must be a credit; for every action there should be an equal and opposite reaction. This is what planning for a secure retirement is all about. Every choice you make now relating to your finances will have an effect on how much you have when you retire.

There is another part of accounting that I also enjoy, which is the creative part of getting numbers to work. This means that although accounting started as a science, it has also become an art. There is an old joke about the only successful candidate for an accounting job. It was the one who correctly answered what appeared to be a very simple question, 'What is one plus one?' The successful candidate's answer was, 'What do you want it to be?'

When it comes to taxation matters it is often all about interpreting the rules to achieve the best result for your client. This is where the creative part of accounting comes in to ensure the facts and a person's finances are organised to match the tax case and benefits you are trying to achieve.

From the simple beginnings of understanding the basic principles of investing—setting goals and budgeting—I went on to experience other importance aspects of investing. Some came from my professional experience, and others came from my personal investing experiences. These included the power of negative gearing and investing in property, and how investing in shares can be extremely rewarding—but shares can also have some major downsides.

It is my personal investing experiences, and the professional experience of advising clients on matters of tax and investing, that have provided the knowledge and reason for writing this book. Professionally I have always been amazed by how many people do not care about their financial future.

I've also been troubled by the willingness of people to be led like lambs to the slaughter when it comes to getting advice from commission-driven salespeople masquerading as advisers. Even when people are given the information that shows a better way of doing things, they keep doing the same things or following the advice of someone who has a vested interest in the advice.

The main problem with the current system of financial advice is that too often the actual cost to the investor is hidden amongst reams of paper. As a fee-for-service professional adviser, when I am trying to interest clients in having a tax and retirement plan prepared, I have seen clients decline the offer of help with the main reason being the cost of the advice. Unfortunately too many people concentrate on the cost of advice rather than comparing the cost with the possible benefit.

To my great disappointment there have been numerous cases where clients have been sold financial planning advice by a commission-based adviser who, on the surface, has appeared cheap. In nearly all of these cases this advice was not as thorough or tax effective, and cost them significantly more than if they had gone to a fee-for-service professional adviser.

Professional note

An example of this was a couple in their early seventies. They had considerable amounts of money invested in term deposits, and a large property that they farmed. As a result of earning substantial interest on their term deposits, they were faced with a large tax bill.

I advised them that they should consider centralising their financial assets in a super fund (this was before the new superannuation system had been introduced, with the even more generous tax benefits available now) and I could prepare a tax and retirement strategy to achieve this. It would take into account all of their retirement and lifestyle goals, and make sure their tax burden was reduced. The plan was also going to address a capital gains tax problem they would face when they were ready to sell their farm. As a result of the considerable assets they had, this was not going to be a simple or uncomplicated plan.

I gave the couple an estimate of $4000 to $5000 for the cost of reviewing their financial and tax situation, and preparing a financial plan. They chose not to proceed, as they believed the plan was too expensive.

It is an understatement to say I was surprised when I prepared next year's tax return for them and found that they had received advice from their bank financial adviser.

> I was pleased to see that the bank adviser had at least convinced them to contribute money to a superannuation fund. I was, however, concerned when I realised that the advice had cost them $15 000 as an entry commission. The super fund they had been put into, as a result of trailing commissions and high administration fees, was also costing them $3000 to $4000 a year more than the fund I would have recommended.
>
> I advised them of what the plan had actually cost them, and how much their super fund was costing them in extra fees every year. I told them I could do some research and provide them with an alternative super fund with a wider choice of investments at a considerably lower cost.
>
> They said they were interested and I quickly came back with another superannuation fund that would save them $4000 a year in fees, and also offer them more investment options. The problem was it would cost approximately $500 to prepare the paperwork to switch them into the new fund. The clients chose to ignore this recommendation, and they stayed with the extremely expensive super fund that they had been put into by the bank adviser.

For this couple, as they were over 65, superannuation was definitely the best option for funding their retirement. People who want to retire before they can access their super need to consider other strategies. Chapter 6 details the various funding strategies that apply throughout a person's life both inside and outside super.

If you understand investing and the various strategies you can use to achieve a financially secure retirement, you won't be blinded by the bull dust often produced under the guise of financial planning advice. This book is all about helping you find gold dust rather than being buried in bull dust.

This also brings me to another important fact about planning for your retirement: without some sacrifice and financial pain there can be no gain or achievement of your retirement goals. It is the sacrifices you make today that will make all the difference when you retire.

This does not mean your lifestyle has to suffer. It means not allowing your lifestyle to be dictated by the income you earn, where either all your income gets spent, or only some goes into savings, which get spent anyway. This book is all about finding a balance between the cost of your lifestyle and your income; setting your life and financial goals; and putting in place plans that will ensure you can fund the lifestyle you want in retirement.

CHAPTER 1

The history of funding your retirement

Before taking a look at the history of retirement, and how people have provided, planned and funded their retirement, it is important to define what retirement is. *Webster's Dictionary* defines retirement as 'a withdrawal from one's position or occupation or from an active working life'.

In practical terms, retirement means different things to different people. An essential aspect of retirement is that it is a time when a person ceases to do the work they have previously done. This means that once a person retires, their living requirements are not funded predominantly from their employment earnings, but from their accumulated investments or from government financial support.

The level of government support or the total value of accumulated investments required for a satisfactory lifestyle in retirement, will depend on a number of factors. That includes a person's age when they retire; how much income they need in retirement; and whether they cease work altogether, or continue working on a part-time or casual basis.

The history of retirement

Retirement and its funding are, in historical terms, recent events. In ancient times, and even until the 1800s, retirement was not an option, as most people worked until they dropped. The only people who could afford some sort of retirement were the nobility and the extremely wealthy. If people could not work, they were supported by family and friends, or they perished.

The military

The concept of retirement was first linked with military service of one kind or another. In ancient Roman times old soldiers were given land when they had ceased service so that they could provide for themselves.

In Britain during the 1700s some soldiers and sailors were paid pensions in recognition of meritorious acts during their military service. Just as it is today, when the high-paid executives get the big retirement benefits, high-ranking officers were awarded perpetual or hereditary pensions to recognise great military or naval victories. Admiral Horatio Nelson was awarded a perpetual pension of 5000 pounds a year, which he and then his descendants received until 1951.

The earliest example of a retirement pension in America was paid in 1636 by the pilgrims of the Plymouth Colony to a soldier maimed in the course of his duty. One of the next examples of pensions being paid was during the American War of Independence. In an effort to retain the services of officers, a lifetime annuity was authorised by Congress.

Possibly as a taste of things to come for baby boomers, the fledgling nation found that it could not afford to meet this commitment to pay the officers a lifetime pension. Facing a threat of rebellion from their own army, Congress negotiated a settlement that resulted in the officers being paid their full pay for a period of only five years.

Public servants

The next group of people to have their retirement funded by pensions were public servants. In the United States, a superannuation plan was established in 1818 for New Jersey teachers. In Britain, the superannuation acts were passed in 1834 to pay pensions to government employees.

Workers

From the time civil servants first started to receive a pension, it was 44 years before employees benefited from industrial and occupational pension schemes. Australia was ahead of the rest of the world when, in 1862, the Bank of New South Wales established Australia's first super fund for its employees. One of the earliest funds in the United States was established by the U.S. Steel Corporation for its employees in 1911.

The general public

It was not until 1883 that a pension scheme was established for the general public. The place was Germany, and the person responsible was Otto von Bismarck. Worried about the increasing appeal of the communists in his country, Bismarck introduced a government pension for everyone aged over 65.

This could be said to be one of the first cynical acts of a politician. This age limit was far from generous, as very few Germans in the late 1800s reached age 65, and if they did they did not live long afterwards to enjoy the pension.

Setting the retirement age at 65 must have seemed like a good idea, most countries adopted this as the age when citizens could start receiving a government-funded pension. The policy of setting a pension age that few people actually attained changed as a result of the Great Depression. In the US the government needed people to retire earlier than that because too many older workers held on to their jobs, which contributed to higher unemployment among the young. To get older workers to retire, the government had to make sure the pension they received guaranteed a reasonable standard of living. Not wanting the US taxpayer to bear the burden of paying for these pensions Franklin D. Roosevelt had the Social Security Act passed in 1935. This act made workers provide for their own retirement by paying old-age insurance.

Retirement age

The ability to encourage people to retire early, and free up employment places for the next generation, did not really catch on until the era of the baby boomers and some of their parents. Parents of the baby boomers began to appreciate the need to stop work before they dropped, and they started retiring at age 65. Table 1.1 shows US statistics demonstrating that the workforce participation rate of men aged 65 and older declined from 78 per cent in 1880 to less than 20 per cent in 1990.

Baby boomers have taken the concept of retirement to the next level, beginning a move to early retirement. This has seen a large increase in the number of people retiring after turning 55. In addition, with the increased life expectancy people now enjoy (refer to table 23 in the appendix), the financial burden on governments reached the point where eligibility for a government-funded pension will increase to age 67.

Table 1.1: US labour force participation rates of men aged 65 and over, 1850–2000

Year	Labour force participation rate (%)
1850	76.6
1860	76.0
1870	–
1880	78.0
1890	73.8
1900	65.4
1910	58.1
1920	60.1
1930	58.0
1940	43.5
1950	47.0
1960	40.8
1970	35.2
1980	24.7
1990	18.4
2000	17.5

Source: Moen (1987), Costa (1998), Bureau of Labor Statistics.

A relatively new development in retirement is the increasing number of people who provide financially for their own retirement rather than just making do with a government pension. This willingness to take greater control of their financial destiny now means more people want to retire rather than reluctantly ceasing work or being forced to retire.

This drive to provide for your own retirement is further evidence of a change in attitude. Coming from the reality that existed for most people of working until they dropped, we have gone through a semi-vegetative state of just existing after 65, to now embracing an active life in retirement that lasts well into our late seventies and beyond.

"I'm semi-retired."

Source: <www.CartoonStock.com>.

Life today is more about achieving a work–life balance that carries on from a person's working life into retirement. So instead of someone stopping dead in their tracks when they stop working, they now, more than ever, blend their working life into retirement.

Funding retirement

Changing attitudes to retirement have meant more and more people are planning for their retirement rather than just accepting what they end up with. This has led to the growth of not only superannuation in Australia, but also the increasing popularity of self managed super funds (SMSFs).

The superannuation system that developed in Australia was different from systems developed in other countries. Instead of requiring members to take a pension in retirement, the Australian system allows members to withdraw their superannuation benefits as a lump sum. Many people regarded their superannuation as a large lotto or lottery win or inheritance. Upon retiring, a lump sum was taken and the funds were spent on overseas holidays, paying off the mortgage, buying a new car, making gifts to the kids, or generally having a good time. Once the money was gone, the retirees had to be content with receiving the age pension.

It took a change in legislation in 1983 for this attitude to superannuation to change. From 1 July 1983, the taxation of lump sum payments changed. Instead of just having 5 per cent of the lump sum taxed at a person's marginal tax rate, the whole amount was taxed at a rate of at least 15 per cent. Over the next decade and a half, other taxes on superannuation were introduced, and in some cases withdrawn, but the government continued to encourage superannuation to be used to fund retirement by permitting retirees to take a pension instead of a lump sum.

This idea of a person providing for their own retirement, rather than relying on an age pension paid by the government, was given a major boost with the introduction of the superannuation guarantee system (SGS) in Australia from 1 July 1992 for the 1993 financial year. The culmination of all of the changes to superannuation, and what gave it a pre-eminent position in funding retirement, occurred on 1 July 2007, when the simpler superannuation system was introduced that made both lump sum and pension superannuation payments tax-free for people who are age 60 or over.

Planning for retirement has become even more necessary because of increased life expectancy and years spent in retirement, and the higher living standards that most people expect today. Retirement has been transformed from a time of subsisting to a period that is planned for and actually enjoyed. People now have to plan more carefully to maximise their accumulated retirement funds during their working life so they can enjoy the kind of lifestyle they want in retirement.

History of financial planning

With people retiring younger, and realising their retirement funds would have to last longer, the business of financial planning developed to meet their needs. It is hard to pin down exactly when this occurred, but financial planning certification in the US commenced in the very early 1970s.

The oldest and best-known financial planning qualification is that of a certified financial planner (CFP). This designation and qualification started in the US and has since been adopted by many countries, including Australia. Since this first qualification was offered by professional associations, an increasing number of financial planning degrees and diplomas have been developed by universities and other tertiary institutions.

In Australia the designation of financial planner can be traced back to 1849, when a a dealer group was formed under what became AMP. A dealer group is a licensed financial organisation that employs people, or appoints them as authorised representatives, to provide financial advice. From this industry-based origin, starting with insurance companies that have developed into more broadly based financial institutions, the development of financial planning services has continued along these lines ever since.

While financial planners and advisers have been employed by the financial institutions that develop products for investors, such as managed funds and insurance policies, their incomes have been based on commissions paid on the products they have sold rather than for the advice they have provided to clients. This has meant that, over the years, people have received mostly product-based advice, instead of strategic advice.

It has only been in recent years that financial planning has taken on a more professional approach, with planners putting the interests of their clients first, rather than acting as a distribution channel for the financial products of their employers.

One of the main contributors to the development of financial planning as a profession in Australia was the passing of the *Financial Services Reform Act 2001*. This act put the financial planning industry on notice that anyone wanting to give financial advice had to have appropriate qualifications and experience, and either hold a licence or be an authorised representative of a licence holder.

This also meant that, from the late 1990s, other professional groups, such as accountants and solicitors, who advised clients on financial matters were faced with a choice. They could either cease providing specific investment advice or they could obtain the appropriate qualifications. Many individuals chose to become certified financial planners, a designation controlled by the Financial Planning Association of Australia, which is a peak body controlled by members of the financial planning industry. To gain this designation a person must have appropriate experience and complete an approved course of study.

Commissions or fee for service?

When the financial services legislation was introduced, many accountants, including me, who had been providing broad-based tax and financial strategy-based advice, were forced to gain the relevant qualification. This has led to a growing number of planners showing their independence of large financial institutions by charging fees for their services (often described as fee-for-service advice) rather than receiving commissions paid on the basis of products sold.

There has been concern at government level for many years of the poor level of advice consumers were receiving from commission-based advisers. Initially this concern led to the Australian Securities & Investments Commission (ASIC) checking the quality of financial plans prepared by using people who masqueraded as clients requiring financial advice.

Despite some improvement in the quality of advice, there was still a high level of concern about the conflict caused by advisers earning commission from the advice they gave. This has culminated in the federal government proposing legislation banning commissions from 1 July 2012. At the time of writing, this legislation had not yet been introduced into federal Parliament.

Getting the balance right

In addition, the turmoil and uncertainty created by the financial meltdown that started in 2008 has continued. The carefully laid retirement plans of many were thrown into disarray. A large section of the self-funded retired population went from being comfortable to being incredibly anxious about whether their investments would produce enough income or last long enough.

The main lessons to be learned from the global financial crisis (GFC) are those of balance and the need to regularly review your financial situation. Unfortunately too many retirees were caught up in the belief that shares would always give a superior return. This led to many retirees, with more than 80 per cent of their investment portfolio in shares, seeing the value of their retirement assets slashed by up to 50 per cent when stock markets crashed.

Retirees who had taken a more balanced view of investing, and spread their investments across cash, shares, property and fixed interest investments, did not suffer such huge drops in value.

The GFC also showed that investors who were engaged in speculation, rather than long-term investment, suffered the most. Speculating with your investments and holding a large percentage of your assets in shares is a strategy more applicable to younger investors. It can be a recipe for disaster for older investors.

This book aims to show you the difference between speculating and investing for the long term so that you not only accumulate investments to fund your retirement, but also learn strategies to make them last as long as possible.

CHAPTER 2

How to plan for your retirement

Trying to work out how much money you will need to fund your retirement can seem like an impossible task. Like most problems, it cannot be solved completely. You can, however, follow a process that will give you the answers you need.

The first part of the process is to break down the problem into its smallest component parts. When it comes to funding your retirement the questions to ask yourself are:

- What are your financial, lifestyle and retirement goals?
- How much money will you need in retirement?
- What do you own and owe now?
- How much income do you earn after tax?
- How much money do you *need*, not *want*, to fund your lifestyle?

Once you have answered these questions, you need to put in place a plan to achieve your goals—accumulating enough investments to fund your retirement and managing them so they last as long as possible.

Most people don't give much thought to organising their finances and planning for retirement until relatively late in life. Baby boomers are in a worse position than the alphabet generations (generations X and Y) who follow them, who have at least had the benefit of the superannuation guarantee system for most or all of their working lives. There is, however, still a serious question for generations X and Y: will their super be enough?

For baby boomers like me the superannuation guarantee system did not commence until we had been working for many years. It is a financial fact that the earlier you start to divert funds to superannuation, or other financial assets you plan to use for retirement, the more money you will have when you reach retirement.

You will note that I have used the word divert and not accumulate. It is a sad fact of most people's financial lives that whatever income they produce that finds its way into their household is spent. And some people with credit cards spend even more than they earn.

If you look back over the past 10, 20 or 30 years, you were probably earning a lot less income than you are now; you were probably relatively happy and content; and this income funded your lifestyle then. No doubt your income now is considerably higher, but if you have not put in place financial plans for your retirement, the amount you are spending on your lifestyle has no doubt simply increased in proportion to the amount by which your income has increased.

The secret to wealth creation, and maximising the funds you will have in retirement, is all about diverting funds away from the household to where it will achieve your retirement and financial goals. That's why the most important step in this problem-solving process is to work out what your goals are. Without goals you have nothing to aim for, and nothing that provides guidance on whether you spend money on something you want, rather than divert it into wealth creation.

Source: <www.CartoonStock.com>.

What are your financial, lifestyle and retirement goals?

You cannot plan how to fund your retirement in isolation. Plans must be made as a part of working out what your other life and financial goals are. These can include:

- funding private school education for your children
- taking the family on a holiday
- building an investment portfolio
- looking after ailing parents
- pursuing hobbies or sporting passions
- building your dream home
- buying a holiday home
- starting a business

- taking 12 months off and travelling around Australia
- retiring before age 65 and having a lifestyle similar to the one you have now.

The most important part of the wealth creation process is to realise at the start what you want and when you want it.

Professional note

On a number of occasions I have helped reinforce for clients what really matters to them when preparing their wealth creation plans. One example of this is a man who came to me feeling that he was a financial failure, because many of his work colleagues owned rental properties and were clearly better off than he was.

After several meetings, and reviewing all of the relevant financial information, it became clear one of his major expenses was private school fees. When asked, he confirmed that his work colleagues' children went to the local high school. After further discussion he realised his work colleagues had made a decision to invest in rental properties, but he had made the decision to invest in private schooling for his children.

This meant his once-stated aim of being able to afford a rental property changed to not only being able to continue to afford private school fees, but also divert cash currently being wasted into reducing debt and increasing his super.

How much money will you need in retirement?

This is a question that many people think and worry about — especially the baby boomers, as they are the first generation to treat retirement as something to be funded and enjoyed. Previous generations didn't really think about retirement too much — they believed the government would look after them by providing the age pension.

Survey results support the baby boomers' worries about how much money they will need. Recent research has shown that baby boomers will be the first generation to spend their kids' inheritance, and that only 50 per cent of boomers believed their retirement savings would provide sufficient income in retirement.

This concern can be traced back to three main sources:

- the increased affluence baby boomers have experienced throughout their lives compared to their parents
- the lack of thought and planning that baby boomers have put into retirement
- the impact of the GFC, which has seen many people's retirement investments severely reduced.

There are several ways of calculating how much income you will need in retirement. One rough rule of thumb method says you will need 75 per cent of your current income when you retire. Although there is no scientific basis to this method of calculating retirement income, one important point to note is that once a person turns 60 pensions received from superannuation are tax-free. This means you need less income to produce the same amount of after-tax income.

A more accurate method can be used to estimate how much income you will need in retirement. As is the case with most worthwhile things, it requires more work but produces a more accurate result. Under this method, you need to accurately record how much income you require now to support your current lifestyle. How to do this is discussed more extensively later in this chapter.

Once you have worked out your current expenses, you can work out how much they will be in retirement. Some current living costs may not be needed when you retire, including education costs, employment-related costs and home loan repayments. Some costs might increase in retirement, such as travel and health. By projecting your current cost of living forward to your preferred retirement date, after allowing for inflation, you can reasonably estimate the retirement income you will need.

You can also use online financial calculators for the calculation. Once you have entered your desired level of retirement income they will work out how much you will need to fund your desired retirement income; how long your retirement savings will last; and, depending on your current retirement investments, how much you need to invest from now on. If you enter the words 'retirement calculator' into a search engine, you will be given plenty of options.

The main point to keep in mind is that the sooner you establish how much income you want or need in retirement, what your retirement savings are now and when you want to retire, the better chance you will have of putting in place a plan to achieve your desired retirement goals.

The consequences of not planning to fund your retirement will be working until you drop; living off a minimal government pension; or trying to get support from your kids whose inheritance you have spent.

What do you own and owe now?

Once you have worked out where you want to go on your financial journey through life and how much income you will need in retirement, you have to work out where you are now.

You need to determine this before you can start your journey. In financial terms this involves documenting what financial and other assets you have and how much you owe.

There are two types of financial assets that a person will have in their lifetime. The first are lifestyle assets and the second are investment assets.

Lifestyle assets

Lifestyle assets are exactly what their name implies—the assets you have and use for personal purposes—and they should not be taken into account when you are planning for retirement. They include your:

- home
- furniture, fittings and personal possessions
- collectables
- jewellery
- cars
- caravans and boats
- toys, whether motorised or not.

The only time that lifestyle assets can be considered for retirement purposes is when they have outlived their use. For example, if you own a motorbike that you can no longer swing your leg over or keep falling off, it could be converted into funds for retirement or to purchase another toy, such as a motorised walking frame.

One of the few times a family home can be included as a financial asset is when the kids have left the nest and you want to down size to something more manageable. The older a person gets the more this becomes a reality, and it can be important to plan for selling your home. For example, if this decision is made when someone is 66, has finished work and produces excess funds from selling their home, unless they meet the 40-hour work test (discussed in chapter 3) this money cannot be contributed to a super fund. If instead the decision had been made before they turned 65, up to $900 000 can be contributed by a couple to superannuation and end up as a tax-free superannuation benefit.

If you do not have some of these lifestyle assets, acquiring them can become a goal that is considered in a wealth creation plan. In this case funds need to be produced so these assets, such as a caravan and a new car, can be purchased.

Financial assets

Financial assets are the assets a person builds up over their lifetime in one form or another. The major asset for funding your retirement should be superannuation. If you plan on retiring before you reach the age at which you can access superannuation, or are investing for other purposes and not just for retirement, other investments must be considered. The other financial assets you build up outside of superannuation can include:

- rental properties
- shares
- managed fund investments
- cash and term deposits
- insurance bonds.

Liabilities

The next thing to document is how much money you owe and to whom you owe it. These debts are split into the two categories of personal private loans and financial investment loans.

Private loans can include:

- a home mortgage
- personal loans
- credit cards for private expenses
- leases and hire-purchase contracts for private-use assets
- amounts borrowed from family and friends for personal reasons.

Financial and investment loans cover all borrowings taken out to purchase investments or that relate to your employment or business. These include:

- a mortgage for an investment property
- a margin facility used to purchase shares or managed investments
- finance used to purchase a work vehicle or business asset.

It is important to highlight a fact when it comes to the tax deductibility of interest on a loan. The overriding factor that determines whether the interest on a loan is tax deductible is not the nature of the property used as security, but the purpose the funds have been used for.

This means if a person uses an existing residence as security for a loan to purchase a new home to live in, and then rents out the old property, the interest on the new loan is not tax deductible against the rent produced. But if a person's home is used as security for a loan to purchase an investment property, the interest will be tax deductible.

A golden rule of borrowing is to pay cash for private expenses and borrow for business or investment purposes.

One of the objects of planning for your retirement is to reduce your personal non–tax deductible debt as quickly as possible. When it comes to a choice between paying off a financial debt, or a private debt, the financial debt should in most cases be paid last.

Wealth creation tip

If credit cards have become a problem and have been maxed out, cut up all but one of them. This credit card is then frozen in an ice-cream container of water and kept in the freezer. This will mean impulse purchases cannot be made, but in the event of an emergency the credit card can be thawed out and used.

How much income do you earn after tax?

At this stage in the funding your retirement process you will have worked out what your goals are, how much income you will need in retirement, and what you own and what you owe. The next step in achieving your financial and retirement goals is to document what income you are earning and how much tax you are paying.

For most people their primary source of income will be from employment or their business. Other sources of income can include:

- interest
- dividends
- government allowances and pensions
- distributions from trusts and partnerships
- foreign income.

Once you have accounted for all of your sources of income you need to work out which of your costs relating to these sources are tax deductible. These can be costs associated with your employment or business, investment costs, donations, tax advice and fees for preparing income tax returns, income protection insurance and deductible superannuation for the self-employed.

After the tax-deductible costs have been totalled and deducted from your income, you will arrive at your taxable income and can calculate how much tax is payable. A short cut is looking at your most recent income tax return. This will have all of the information and, if prepared by a professional, will also have an estimate of your tax payable. Chapter 4 discusses income tax in more detail.

You will now know what after-tax income you are producing as an individual or as a couple. From here we go to the final step in preparing for the wealth creation process: working out how much you spend now and what is left that can be diverted into wealth creation before it is spent.

How much money do you *need*, not *want*, to fund your lifestyle?

A common feature of most people's personal financial situation is that the money they earn gets spent. A major part of wealth creation is controlling what gets spent and where, rather than allowing the amount of income you earn to dictate what you spend. Unless you are prepared to endure some pain today, you will never maximise your retirement funding gain. This pain comes in the form of taking the time and effort to work out where your money currently goes.

Professional note

Many times when I have been preparing wealth creation plans for people, due to the effort that is required in preparing a domestic expenditure budget, I am asked if it is really necessary. After having confirmed that the effort will be worthwhile, I never cease to be amazed that, after putting the effort into working out what they currently spend their money on, most people finally get an understanding of just how much of the money is slipping through their fingers.

Recently I was developing a wealth creation plan for a couple in which the husband wanted to leave his current employment to wind down in preparation for retirement. They prepared a generous household expenditure budget and it soon became clear that their after-tax income exceeded their expenses by more than $20000 a year. This meant $20000 a year, which could have been diverted into wealth creation without their lifestyle suffering, was being spent on living expenses that they couldn't properly account for.

The first step in preparing a household expenditure budget is to divide the types of expenses into two categories: non-discretionary costs (which include all necessary expenses) and discretionary costs (which often vary in proportion to a person's income). Non-discretionary expenses include the following:

- *home and residence*: all the costs that relate to where you live, including rent or mortgage repayments, and other ongoing costs, such as electricity, gas and council rates
- *living*: all the costs related to keeping the family fed, clothed and looking good
- *loan repayments*: all the other non–tax deductible forms of finance commitments, including personal loans, hire purchases and credit cards

- *health*: all medical, hospital and other associated health costs, including health insurance
- *education*: education costs for children as well as the parents
- *transport*: all costs related to motor vehicles and other conveyances, such as taxis and public transport
- *insurance*: all non–tax deductible types of insurance, including contents and life insurance
- *miscellaneous*: can include such things as child support payments and expenses related to pets.

Discretionary expenses include the following:

- alcohol and cigarettes
- dining out
- entertainment, such as movies
- holidays
- sports, hobbies and other recreational pursuits
- magazine and other subscriptions
- gifts for birthdays, Christmas and other occasions.

When preparing your household expenditure budget, it is important not to be too mean in estimating how much you want or need to spend. If your budget is too thrifty you may diminish your lifestyle so much that the financial and personal pain is too great, and because the financial gain can seem too far away, you will abandon your plan and go back to your income dictating what you spend.

As a guide to judge your own expenditure levels take a look at table 2.1 (overleaf), which was produced by the Australian Bureau of Statistics after conducting its last household expenditure survey in 2004.

Table 2.1: household expenditure across income groups according to the 2004 Australian Bureau of Statistics survey

| | Income groupings | | | | | | |
	Lowest ($)	Second ($)	Third ($)	Fourth ($)	Highest ($)	Average ($)
Mean gross household income per week	263	555	930	1385	2512	1128
Weekly household expenditure						
Housing costs, including rent, mortgage, rates, repairs	77	101	152	168	221	144
Domestic fuel and power	17	20	24	26	32	24
Food and non-alcoholic beverages	65	89	106	130	164	111
Meals out and fast foods	13	23	40	52	84	42
Alcoholic beverages	9	14	23	27	44	23
Tobacco products	7	11	13	14	12	12
Clothing and footwear	13	20	31	46	67	35
Household furnishings and equipment	25	36	51	62	86	52
Household services	15	19	24	32	46	27
Telephone and facsimile charges	16	21	28	31	40	27

	Income groupings					
	Lowest ($)	Second ($)	Third ($)	Fourth ($)	Highest ($)	Average ($)
Medical care and health expenses	22	32	46	53	77	46
Transport	57	90	134	184	231	139
Recreational and educational equipment	16	25	37	56	75	42
Recreational fees and charges	11	19	25	37	54	29
Holidays	12	24	28	38	72	35
Animal expenses	4	8	10	12	12	9
Personal care	7	11	15	21	32	17
Miscellaneous goods	7	9	13	19	23	14
Miscellaneous services	21	33	61	84	129	65
Total goods and services expenditure	**413**	**604**	**859**	**1090**	**1499**	**893**

Source: Abridged from <www.abs.gov.au/AUSSTATS/abs@.nsf/DetailsPage/6535.0.55.0012003-04%20(Reissue)?0penDocument>.

Note: All figures have been rounded to the nearest dollar.

A new survey was conducted through the 2010 year but results will not be available until late 2011. The 2004 results are helpful on two levels. The first is to provide a guide for you to compare your estimated expenditure against. The second is to demonstrate that even with a proper survey people find it hard to estimate their expenditure. This is evidenced by the fact that the total living costs for the two lowest income groups exceeds their income.

These results should only be used as a guide and need to be adjusted to reflect inflation over this time. Also some expenditure items will have decreased, some will be new and some will have increased, such as internet and computer costs.

Conclusion

At this stage of putting a plan together to fund your retirement you should now know:

- the total value of your lifestyle assets
- the total value of your investment assets
- what debts you have split between personal and investment loans
- how much income you are earning after tax
- how much of your income is needed to meet your lifestyle living expenses
- what excess cash could be produced if you are disciplined enough to stick to your domestic household expenditure budget.

From here you can start to apply the various wealth creation strategies that will ensure you maximise the investments you need for retirement, while at the same time helping to limit the amount of income tax you are paying.

Some of these wealth creation strategies are:

- debt consolidation
- salary sacrifice
- interest-only payments on investment loans
- super splitting with a spouse
- tax-effective investments
- negative-geared investments
- transition to retirement pensions
- non-concessional super contributions
- timing capital gains to reduce the amount of capital gains tax payable by making self-employed, tax-deductible superannuation contributions
- ensuring your superannuation fund is working for you
- structuring your employment income tax effectively.

All of these strategies are effective on a number of levels. On one level they achieve the all-important result of diverting income away from the household so it can be invested for the long term.

On another level they use the laws relating to super-annuation, retirement, taxation and Centrelink payments to maximise the investment benefit and increase the value of assets you will have to help fund your retirement, while ensuring you are not paying more tax than you have to. For that reason it is important to have a basic understanding of the various laws that affect the income you and your investments earn, how you can accumulate various investments and receive an income in retirement that is not only tax effective but also ensures your retirement investments last as long as you do.

CHAPTER 3

The retirement rules

Before embarking on the wealth creation strategies that will help fund your retirement it is important to get a basic understanding of the rules relating to retirement. These include the income tax and superannuation regulations, as well as Centrelink's tests and rules associated with payment of the age pension.

These rules are based on complicated pieces of legislation and regulations, so I will be trying to give you the gist of the law rather than the letter of the law. What follows in this chapter and chapter 4 should be used only as a guide: if you need help with a particular tax, superannuation or Centrelink problem, you should seek professional advice.

Superannuation is one of the most tax-effective ways to generate an income in retirement, so it's an important part of wealth creation. It is important not only to know when you can access your superannuation, but also when and how much you can contribute to superannuation.

Some people will want to retire before they are allowed to access their superannuation. In these circumstances strategies need to be developed so that their investments outside superannuation will either produce sufficient income, or can be sold to produce cash, to fund the desired lifestyle after retirement.

Accessing superannuation

When it comes to accessing superannuation, given that the main purpose of superannuation is to provide an income in retirement, people need to meet a condition of release before the trustee of their super fund will pay out their super benefit. The exception to this was the transition to retirement pension introduced under the Howard government. This pension allows someone who has reached preservation age to access their super in the form of a pension while remaining in the workforce.

Preservation age

The major qualification for accessing superannuation is reaching what is known as your preservation age. For people born before 1 July 1960, preservation age is 55. For those born on or after that date the preservation age gradually increases to 60, as is shown in table 3.1.

Table 3.1: when you can access your super — the preservation ages

Date of birth	Preservation age
1 July 1960 to 30 June 1961	56
1 July 1961 to 30 June 1962	57
1 July 1962 to 30 June 1963	58
1 July 1963 to 30 June 1964	59
After 30 June 1964	60

Ages 55 to 59: the intention to retire

Once you reach preservation age, and meet a condition of release, you can take all of your superannuation in the form of a lump sum or a pension. People aged between 55 and

59 must retire from full-time work if they want to access their super. In technical terms this means the person does not intend to work more than 10 hours a week.

Professional note

This intention to retire from full-time work is exactly that, an intention rather than a long-term, inflexible requirement. There have been many cases of people intending to retire from full-time work, but for some reason or another have ended up working more than 10 hours a week.

There are many examples of this among people who retired before the GFC in 2008 and saw the value of their retirement investments slashed. Many had to go back to work so they could reduce the income they needed to take from their superannuation assets so they didn't have to sell investments to produce the income they needed to fund their lifestyle.

I have a client who ran his own business and had accumulated a large self managed super fund. One of the assets in the super fund was a property. His intention had always been to retire at age 60 and take a lump sum payment in the form of the property being transferred into his name.

After doing this and starting to renovate the property, the manager my client had hired to run his business resigned. This meant after three months he had to come out of retirement and run his business until he could find a replacement manager.

Despite the fact that he was now working more than 10 hours a week, his *intention* had always been to retire. Even though he had to go back to working full-time due to circumstances beyond his control, he still met the condition of release.

Ages 60 to 65

For people aged from 60 to 64, an extra condition of release makes it easier to access superannuation. People in this age bracket only need to cease employment with an employer to meet a condition of release. This means a person working in a full-time job and a part-time job could give up either job, meet a condition of release, and have access to their super.

Once a person turns 65 they have unfettered access to all of their superannuation, even if they are still working full-time.

Other conditions of release

The other conditions of release for super that can be planned for as a part of your retirement funding strategies are:

- permanent disablement
- terminal illness
- death
- taking a transition to retirement pension.

Having insurance within your super fund can cover you for the first three events, and can be a strategy for planning your retirement income. Insurance cover will help fund a payout should one of these unfortunate circumstances arise.

People who meet a condition of release, except for those choosing a transition to retirement pension, can take either a lump sum or a pension. No maximum limits are placed on lump sums, but there are minimum rates that must be paid as pensions, as shown in table 3.2.

Table 3.2: minimum pension rates for ages 55 to 95 plus

Age range	Minimum pension (percentage of account balance)
55–64	4
65–74	5
75–79	6
80–84	7
85–89	9
90–94	11
95 and over	14

A person qualifies for a transition to retirement pension if they are still working and have reached their preservation age. Transition to retirement pensions have a maximum pension rate payable of 10 per cent of a person's account balance in a super fund, in addition to the minimum pension rate.

Contributing to superannuation

Like most things to do with superannuation, who can contribute to superannuation and the maximum levels of contribution, depend on a person's age.

To be able to contribute to superannuation, people aged 65 to 74 must pass a work test, which means they have to work in paid employment for at least 40 hours in a consecutive 30-day period in the financial year in which the super contribution is made.

Anyone under the age of 65 can make both concessional (tax-deductible, or before-tax) and non-concessional (after-tax) contributions. There are upper limits for both types of contributions. For people aged less than 50, the maximum contribution limit in 2011 is $25 000 per year. For those aged 50 and above, the maximum limit is $50 000 per year until 1 July 2012, when it will reduce to $25 000.

The federal Labor government made an election promise in 2010 to retain the maximum contribution limit of $50 000 after 2012 for people who are aged over 50 and have less than $500 000 in superannuation. The limits had not been changed at the time of writing.

Wealth creation tip

If this new contribution limit becomes law, and one member of a couple has a large superannuation balance, they should consider splitting their superannuation with their spouse. This will mean for as long as possible their super will remain below $500 000 and they can still each contribute up to the $50 000 limit each year.

The two types of concessional, or deductible, contributions are employer contributions and self-employed contributions. To qualify to make a self-employed super contribution a person must either not be employed, thus receiving no super contributions from an employer, or their employment income must be less than 10 per cent of their total taxable income.

For non-concessional (after-tax) contributions the yearly limit for everyone is $150 000. People who are younger than 65 can bring forward up to two years of non-concessional contributions, resulting in a maximum contribution in one year of $450 000. If a fund member uses this strategy, no non-concessional contributions can be made in the following two years.

Tax planning tip

The ability to contribute up to $450 000 a year to super does not stop when someone turns 65. They can contribute the $450 000 in the financial year in which they turn 65, provided they have not exceeded the contribution level in the three previous years.

Both concessional and non-concessional contribution levels are meant to increase each year in accordance with increases in average weekly ordinary times earnings (AWOTE). The non-concessional contribution level is set at six times the under-50 concessional limit. Unfortunately the increases in these contribution levels are made in increments of $5000. As a result of the under-50 concessional limit being halved — originally it was set at $50 000 in 2007 and was then reduced by the Rudd Labor government for the 2009 year down to $25 000 — neither contribution level has increased since then, and it is hard to predict when they will.

Taxation rules and retirement

Most of the taxation rules relating to retirement concern the tax rates payable on retirement income (pensions) and lump sums. The most tax-effective way to receive an income in retirement is from a superannuation fund. Tax offsets may also apply to help reduce the tax burden when income in retirement comes from outside of superannuation. The combination of these two facts means you need to earn less income to produce a required amount of money to fund your retirement.

Tax on components of superannuation

A superannuation benefit can be made up of a number of components, which are taxed differently. There are two main types of benefits, and three sub-categories of benefits, that can make up a person's superannuation balance. The two main types of benefits are taxable benefits and non-taxable, or tax-free, benefits.

Taxable benefits

Taxable benefits are made up of concessional contributions and income earned by the superannuation fund that has been credited to the member's account.

The taxable component is calculated by subtracting the total of a member's tax-free benefits from the total value of their superannuation. The value of taxable benefits generally increases as a result of concessional contributions and a person's share of the net income made by the fund each year. The value decreases as a result of benefits paid out or when there is negative income or a loss is made. A loss can occur when administration costs and investment losses exceed investment income, or the value of the member's investments decrease, such as happened through the GFC, and a large, unrealised loss is made on the investments.

Unrealised losses occur because a super fund's investments are valued at market value. This means due to investment markets rising and falling the value of investments also rises and falls. A loss is not actually experienced until the investment is sold, which means when an investment drops from what it was valued at the previous year there is an unrealised loss.

Tax-free benefits

Tax-free benefits are made up of non-concessional contributions, in other words made from after-tax earnings and a tax deduction is not claimed by the person making the contribution. These benefits can be paid from the super fund without any additional tax being paid. These benefits can also include the value of a person's superannuation account at 1 July 2007 that related to their pre-1983 service; undeducted, or non-concessional, contributions paid into the fund; contributions made from the sale of business assets by a small business owner who has claimed the small business retirement exemption; and invalidity payments made after June 1994.

When a person is in the accumulation phase — that is, when they are contributing to super in preparation for retirement — the value of their tax-free benefits increases as a result of new non-concessional contributions being made, or from small business capital gains tax exempt retirement contributions. The value decreases when benefits are paid to a member. Once a super fund starts paying a pension to a member, the member's tax-free benefits percentage is locked in and stays the same for as long as the pension is paid.

Sub-categories of benefit

There are three sub-categories of superannuation benefits that dictate whether a benefit can be taken at any time, or a condition of release must be met. They are preserved benefits, restricted non-preserved benefits and unrestricted non-preserved benefits.

Preserved benefits

Since 1 July 1999 all super contributions for members aged under 65, and income earned by a fund on their super accounts, are preserved. This means that unless a member has met a condition of release previously, all of their benefits from that date will be preserved. Preserved benefits are not accessible by a member until they meet a condition of release.

Restricted non-preserved benefits

Few people have restricted non-preserved benefits. They include non-concessional (or undeducted) contributions made before 1 July 1999 and benefits accumulated in certain sponsored super funds established before 22 December 1986. These benefits can't be withdrawn until a condition of release has been met that does not have a cashing restriction.

Unrestricted non-preserved benefits

Unrestricted non-preserved benefits are benefits that have remained in a super fund after a member has met a condition of release and no cashing restriction applies. A member can withdraw these from the fund at any time.

Lump sum or pension?

Superannuation can be paid in two forms: as a lump sum or as a pension. The tax treatment differs for each of these payments, depending on when they are received and what type of benefits make up the payments.

For someone aged 60 or more, all payments from a superannuation fund are exempt from tax. When someone is aged under 60, no tax is payable on the tax-free benefits. The taxation treatment of taxable benefits differs depending on when they are paid.

The tax treatment also differs between payments from a taxed fund and payments from an untaxed fund. Most Australians have their superannuation in taxed super funds.

The people most likely to receive superannuation benefits from an untaxed fund are those who have been employed by a federal or state government body. Death benefits paid by a super fund from insurance proceeds are also classed as untaxed benefits.

Lump sum payments

Lump sum superannuation payments can only be made if a member meets a condition of release. The taxation of these payments differs according to the type of payment and the age of the person receiving it. Where a person's taxable income exceeds the threshold, the Medicare levy of 1.5 per cent is also payable.

Retirement benefits

To receive a retirement benefit, the condition of release you must meet is that you must be retiring from the workforce. A person's age of retirement depends on when they were born and their personal circumstances.

Age less than 55

It is unusual for someone under 55 to be able to gain access to superannuation. The exception is if they have unrestricted non-preserved benefits in their superannuation fund, or they have been classed as permanently disabled. The maximum rate of tax on a taxable lump sum is 20 per cent. As this is a maximum rate, for someone with little to no other taxable income, some or all of the benefit paid may be taxed at the lowest tax rate of 15 per cent, and after the low income tax offset (LITO) is applied, no tax may be payable.

For example, if someone received a taxable lump sum of $15 000 due to being disabled, and received no other income in that year, no tax would be payable as the LITO would exceed the tax payable.

Super can also be paid to a member aged under 55 if they experience severe financial hardship. If a super fund member dies, their benefit will also be paid out according to super fund rules. These conditions of release are described on p. 43.

Age 55 to 59

Fund members can receive their super benefit when they reach their preservation age, between ages 55 and 59. The tax payable by members in this age bracket is split into two components. The first is tax-free up to the low rate lump sum limit, and the second is the excess that is taxed at a maximum rate of 15 per cent plus the Medicare levy.

A tax-free threshold also applies. It is a lifetime limit on the lump sums that can be received tax-free. It increases in line with increases in AWOTE, in $5000 increments. The limits for the current and past year are shown in table 3.3.

Table 3.3: lifetime limits on lump sums for 2009–10 and 2010–11

Income year	Limit
2010–11	$160 000
2009–10	$150 000

The tax-free limit applies to a person for life. The ATO keeps track of all taxable lump sum super payouts a person receives. Once a person exceeds the tax-free limit, tax has to be paid in the year they receive the excess. This can mean that if the lump sum is large enough, tax may be paid the first time a person receives a lump sum. If relatively small lump sum amounts are taken, several years can go by before a lump sum becomes taxable.

Permanent disability payouts

For people who have reached their preservation age and are eligible to receive these payouts the amount received is exempt from tax. These payouts are therefore tax-free.

Temporary disability payouts

Temporary disability payouts are classed as replacement income and are taxed at a person's applicable marginal tax rate.

Death benefits

A member's superannuation, and any insurance payment they are entitled to, is paid out if they die. Death benefits are tax-free when received by dependants, but tax is payable at a rate of 15 per cent when received by non-dependants on taxable benefits and at 30 per cent on untaxed benefits. The definition of dependants for income tax purposes includes:

- current spouse
- former spouse
- de facto partner
- any child
- any person who has an interdependency relationship with the super fund member.

A child can also include children from a marriage, those who have been adopted, stepchildren and those born out of wedlock. Non-dependants, such as adult children, who receive a taxable benefit from a super fund pay tax on the super received at 16.5 per cent (15 per cent plus the Medicare levy).

Pension payments

With the commencement of a superannuation pension made up of both taxable and tax-free benefits, the percentage of each component is calculated. The percentage relating to each component stays the same for as long as the pension is paid. Tax is only ever payable on the taxable portion of pension benefits received.

Age less than 55

Superannuation pensions received are treated like any other income. Tax is paid by the person receiving the pension at their marginal tax rate, plus the Medicare levy.

Age 55 to 59

The taxable component of a superannuation pension received is taxed at the applicable marginal rate of tax reduced by a 15 per cent tax offset. This means the highest rate of tax and Medicare levy payable on a super pension for people in this age bracket is 31.5 per cent.

Centrelink benefits

Eligibility for virtually every Centrelink benefit is based on passing various tests or meeting certain criteria. In addition to the age pension, these benefits include disability support pensions, carer's payments, and Youth and Newstart allowances. For the sake of this book I will concentrate on the tests and criteria for the age pension.

Before discussing Centrelink benefits in greater detail I am hoping that this section of the book will be of no benefit to you at all. This will be because your wealth creation strategies will have been so successful that you are well and truly funding your own retirement and will never be eligible to receive the age pension.

Despite this wish, eligibility for the age pension can play an important part in ensuring a person's retirement income is supplemented so that their retirement investments last for as long as possible.

However, for many Australians, especially for the generation preceding the baby boomers, their number one goal has been to become eligible to receive the age pension. On one level this stems from the belief that after having paid taxes for so many years, they are entitled to receive something back. On a purely financial level, eligibility to receive even one dollar in Centrelink benefits makes the recipient eligible for many of the concessions that pensioners receive.

Professional note

I have a client whose tax and financial affairs I have been looking after for almost 30 years. He made it clear almost from day one that he wanted to become eligible to receive the age pension.

For many of my clients this would not have been too great a challenge, but this person had run several successful businesses in his time and also invested very heavily in property, which meant the task was almost impossible. Over many years I had tried to convince him of the benefits of superannuation when it came to providing income in retirement. This was even before the major changes that occurred on 1 July 2007.

His attitude, like that of many of his generation, was he didn't trust superannuation. To loosely quote him: 'I don't trust the government, as soon as I put my money into superannuation they will tax it out of existence'.

After many years I finally convinced him, as a result of some extremely large capital gains tax bills, to put almost $1 million into superannuation.

For many people the huge drop in the value of their retirement investments at the start of the GFC was nothing short of catastrophic. Just as it did for everyone else, the value of my client's superannuation also decreased, but as the old saying goes, 'One man's meat is another man's poison'.

With the total value of his assets dropping it meant they fell below the maximum limit of the assets test for the age pension, and he finally became eligible to receive it. I have never ever seen anyone happier that their investments had dropped almost 20 per cent in value. The bad news for my client is that his retirement assets will eventually increase and he once again will be ineligible for the age pension.

There are three tests for eligibility for the age pension. These are based on the applicant's age, the assets they own, and their income. A person's eligibility to receive an age pension is affected by whichever of the assets and income tests produces the greatest reduction. This means if the assets test results in a small amount of age pension being received, while the income test results in no age pension being received, the income test will apply.

A brief summary of the major tests for eligibility for a Centrelink age pension follows. However, this is a complicated area of law and, before taking any actions, you should seek professional advice.

The age test

The first hurdle someone faces for eligibility for the age pension is reaching age-pension age. When the age pension was first introduced men had to wait until they were age 65, while women became eligible at age 60.

This may seem peculiar given that women have tended statistically to outlive men. However, this wasn't actually generous towards women, as the income test relates to the income earned by a couple, so if their husband was still working the income test meant a 60-year-old female could not receive the age pension.

In the continuing search to balance the nation's budget, the age at which people become eligible for a pension has been increased. The initial change increased the eligibility age for females from 60 to 65, to match males.

A second change, which will apply from 1 July 2017, will gradually increase the age of eligibility from 65 to 67. These increases are shown in table 3.4 (overleaf).

Table 3.4: eligibility for age pension by age for men and women

Born	Women eligible for age pension at age	Men eligible for age pension at age
Before 1 July 1935	60.0	65.0
Between 1 July 1935 and 31 December 1936	60.5	65.0
Between 1 January 1937 and 30 June 1938	61.0	65.0
Between 1 July 1938 and 31 December 1939	61.5	65.0
Between 1 January 1940 and 30 June 1941	62.0	65.0
Between 1 July 1941 and 31 December 1942	62.5	65.0
Between 1 January 1943 and 30 June 1944	63.0	65.0
Between 1 July 1944 and 31 December 1945	63.5	65.0
Between 1 January 1946 and 30 June 1947	64.0	65.0
Between 1 July 1947 and 31 December 1948	64.5	65.0
Between 1 January 1949 and 30 June 1952	65.0	65.0
Between 1 July 1952 and 31 December 1953	65.5	65.5
Between 1 January 1954 and 30 June 1955	66.0	66.0
Between 1 July 1955 and 31 December 1956	66.5	66.5
After 1 January 1957	67.0	67.0

The assets test

Under the assets test the total value of an individual's or a couple's assets is calculated. When the total value of these assets is below a low asset threshold, applicants receive the full age pension. If the total value exceeds the threshold, the pension is reduced on a graduated scale until no pension is paid.

There are two assets test limits, one applies to homeowners and the other applies to non-homeowners, as shown in table 3.5. Another assets test applies to a couple who are separated due to illness. It has the same lower limit as a couple, but a much higher upper limit applies before they lose the pension. In addition, where only one member of a couple is eligible for the age pension, the couple assets tests limits apply.

Table 3.5: eligibility for age pension—assets test thresholds

Family situation	Lower limit		Upper limit	
	Homeowner	Non-homeowner	Homeowner	Non-homeowner
Single	$181750	$313250	$659250	$790750
Couple (combined)	$258000	$389500	$978000	$1109500

For every $1000 in total assets that exceeds the lower limit, the fortnightly pension rate is reduced by $1.50 until the upper limit is reached, at which point no pension is paid. The lower limit is increased annually, while the upper limit increases annually when the fortnightly pension rate is increased every six months in March and September.

Assets counted in this test are virtually everything a person owns, including household contents, cars, caravans, and investments, including superannuation and cash. The value that must be placed on all of these assets is the current market value.

For assets such as cars and household contents the value for Centrelink assets test purposes is often a lot less than they cost. For example, Centrelink allows people to value household contents at a lower amount than they are insured for. For these it is acceptable to value them at what you would get if you had a garage sale. Where a person is receiving an income stream from a lifetime pension, Centrelink uses a complicated valuation method to place a value on this as an asset.

The assets test also includes assets held overseas converted to an equivalent value in Australian dollars.

Some assets are not counted in the assets test. The prime example of this is a person's home. Where a home is on more than two hectares of land the exemption only applies to two hectares, and the excess land is counted as an asset. Other assets not counted in the assets test include:

- an interest in a granny flat where the amount paid for the flat is greater than the difference between the homeowner and non-homeowner allowable assets levels
- any interest in a deceased estate before the estate is finalised
- any medal or decoration for valour, as long as it is not held for investment or hobby purposes
- aids for disabled people
- a gift car provided by the Department of Veterans Affairs
- the value of any accommodation bond paid for hostel accommodation
- the value of all superannuation or amounts in rollover funds if you are under age pension age

- the value of a cemetery plot for you or your partner
- prepaid funeral expenses or up to two funeral investment bonds costing up to $11 000 in total.

If you have sold your home, and you are planning to use the proceeds to buy another home, the proceeds of the sale will also be exempt from the assets test for up to 12 months. If delays beyond a person's control are experienced, this exemption can be extended for up to an additional 12 months.

Gifts

Individuals can't escape the assets test by giving away assets or cash as gifts unless they are below a prescribed value. Two thresholds are set to limit how much a person can give. The first is $10 000 a year for either a single person or couple. The second is the total value of gifts an individual or a couple can make over a rolling five-year period of up to $30 000. Gifts include assets and money transferred to anybody for no value, or for less than their market value.

Gifts that exceed these two thresholds—anything above $10 000 in a single year or $30 000 in a five-year period— will be counted as an asset under the assets test and possibly counted by the deeming rules (discussed on p. 53) under the income test. These excess gifts will continue to be counted under these tests until the fifth anniversary of the date of the gift.

The income test

In addition to the assets test, anyone applying for an age pension must pass the income test. Two levels of income apply, depending on an applicant's personal situation. The income thresholds are shown in table 3.6 (overleaf).

Table 3.6: eligibility for age pension — income test thresholds

Family situation	Lower threshold $ per fortnight	Upper threshold $ per fortnight
Single	Up to 146.0	1578.20
Couple (combined)	Up to 256.0	2415.20
Couple separated due to illness (combined)	Up to 256.0	3120.40

Where a person's income exceeds the minimum threshold their fortnightly pension is reduced by 50 cents in the dollar of the excess income earned for a single person, and 25 cents in the dollar each for both members of a couple. Once a person's income from any source other than the age pension exceeds the upper threshold, no age pension is paid.

This income test was introduced on 20 September 2009. Transitional arrangements were introduced at that time to ensure no existing pensioner would be worse off as a result of the changes. These transitional rules use the old reduction factor, of 40 cents in the dollar for single people and 20 cents in the dollar for couples, to calculate the effect on a pension under the income test.

The income test can also have an effect on the various allowance rates paid to age pensioners. Another of the changes introduced on 20 September 2009 was the replacement of various allowances, including the GST supplement and the telephone utilities and pharmaceutical allowances, by a single new pension supplement.

There are in effect three different types of income counted under the income test. These are:

- actual income
- deemed income
- adjusted actual income.

Actual income

Included in the first category are such things as employment income, employment-related fringe benefits, net business income, income distributed from trusts and private companies, amounts of salary sacrificed as super contributions, net rental income, and income received from boarders and lodgers.

Along with other Centrelink changes that were introduced on 20 September 2009, a new work bonus was introduced, which affects the way employment income is treated under the income test. If a person chooses to work past the age of eligibility for the age pension, only half of the first $500 per fortnight of their gross employment income is counted. Income earned from employment in excess of the $500 is treated as ordinary income.

Deemed income

Deemed income was introduced many years ago to stop people artificially decreasing their income from financial investments. Rather than counting the actual income received from financial assets, an income is deemed to be earned. Where a pensioner earns less than the deemed income they are worse off under this system; where they earn more, they are better off.

Investments included as financial assets include the following:

- bank, building society and credit union accounts
- term deposits and debentures
- friendly society bonds
- managed investments
- listed shares and securities

- shares in listed public companies
- gold and other bullion
- superannuation account balances when the member is of pension age
- loans to people and other entities, such as trusts and companies
- proceeds from the sale of a home not counted under the assets test
- amounts gifted above the gifting limits.

Once a total value for all of your financial investments is arrived at, there are two levels of deeming rates applied for singles and another set for couples. The deeming rates for a single person are 3 per cent per year on the first $43 200 of financial assets, and 4.5 per cent per year on the excess. For couples, where at least one person is getting a pension, the deeming rates are 3 per cent per year on the first $72 000 of combined financial assets and 4.5 per cent per year on the excess.

Adjusted actual income

This third category of income relates to types of income where Centrelink reduces the amount of actual income received each year by a percentage of what it regards as a purchase price (they call this the annual deductible purchase price). The most common example of this type of income is a superannuation pension.

A reduction for this purchase price is allowed because it is expected at some time a portion of the original capital value of the superannuation account will be received. This is definitely the case with superannuation pensions, due to the minimum pension payment rates that apply.

The amount of the annual deductible purchase price is calculated by dividing the value of the superannuation account at the time the pension started by the person's life expectancy at that time. In some cases, where a person draws a minimum superannuation pension, deducting the purchase price of the pension results in a large enough reduction in the income for no income to be counted by Centrelink.

An example of how the income and assets tests are applied

How these assets and income tests work is best illustrated by the following example. John is single, has just turned 65, and has the investments and income from those investments shown in table 3.7.

Table 3.7: John's eligibility for the age pension

Asset	Value ($)	Annual income ($)
Exempt assets		
Home	450 000	0
Financial assets		
Listed shares	50 000	2 500
Term deposits	50 000	3 000
Superannuation*	250 000	12 500
Other assets		
Car	10 000	
Household contents	7 000	
Total	367 000	18 000
Employment income†		7 800
Total income		**25 800**

Table 3.7 *(cont'd)*: John's eligibility for the age pension

Asset	Value ($)	Annual income ($)
Assets test		
Value counted		367 000
Less lower limit		181 750
Excess		185 250
Asset test reduction at $1.50 per $1000		278
Income test		
Financial assets counted		100 000
Deemed income at 3% on $43 200		1 296
Deemed income at 4.5% on excess		2 556
Total deemed income		3 852
Superannuation pension	12 500	
Less purchase price*	13 484	
Super pension counted in income test		0
Employment income	7 800	
Less work bonus reduction[†]	3 900	
Net employment income		3 900
Annual deemed income		7 752
Deemed and actual income per fortnight		298
Less lower threshold		146
Excess income		152
Income test reduction at 50% of excess		76

*John commenced his superannuation pension when he had turned 65 when, according to the applicable life expectancy tables, his life expectancy was 18.54 years. The deductible amount of the purchase price has been arrived at by dividing the $250 000 by 18.54.

† As John is eligible for the work bonus, and he is earning less than $500 a fortnight, he is entitled to the full 50 per cent reduction of his employment income.

In John's case, as the assets test produces the biggest reduction in the pension, it will apply. Had John not commenced a pension from his superannuation fund, his deemed income from superannuation would have resulted in an extra $11 250 a year in deemed income. This would have resulted in a reduction under the income test of an extra $216 per fortnight. In this case the income test reduction would be $292 and it would have applied.

Conclusion

At this point you should have enough of an understanding of the rules relating to superannuation and eligibility for a Centrelink age pension. The combination of this information with the taxation information covered in chapter 4 forms the basis for most wealth creation strategies that will help you fund your retirement.

Income tax and your retirement

They say there are two inevitabilities in life: death and taxes. When it comes to funding your retirement the aims are to have as much time as possible between retirement and death, and during your lifetime pay no more taxes than you need to.

This is why when you are preparing a wealth creation plan you need to carefully consider maximising the taxation benefits available in the areas of income tax, capital gains tax (CGT), and the goods and services tax (GST). It is, therefore, important that you have some basic understanding of these taxes.

You are probably wondering how GST can apply to you when you are not running a business. There are times, however, in a person's investing life when the unwary may have to pay GST. For this reason I will start with GST and how it can affect an investor.

Warning: This chapter is meant to be only a guide that will help you make decisions in the future that will result in you achieving a better tax result. When it comes to making decisions about tax, it is important to seek professional advice before making any decisions.

Goods and services tax

Anyone who makes more than $75 000 per year from carrying on an enterprise must be registered for and pay GST. Carrying on an enterprise means where something is done for the purpose of making a profit. Individual investors may not realise that the ATO would recognise some of their activities as enterprises, and so require that they pay GST on their profit. If the ATO finds out that you should have been registered for GST, and you weren't, there can be severe tax consequences.

Two examples are discussed here: subdividing a property, and investing in commercial property.

Example 1: subdividing a property

As a result of local councils allowing the subdivision of large residential blocks, some people have released accumulated wealth in their home without having to move. In the ATO ruling setting out what constitutes carrying on an enterprise, the activity of subdividing land, and building a unit to sell, is classed as carrying on an enterprise.

As most properties have a selling value of more than $75 000 the activity of subdividing land and constructing a building to sell, or demolishing the existing residence and constructing two new buildings and selling one, will result in the owners carrying on an enterprise, as their intention is to make a profit.

However, where a residential property is subdivided and the land is sold, there is no requirement to register for GST. In this case, even though GST will not be payable, the sale could result in a large CGT bill. This is because by subdividing the land a new asset is created that is distinct from the house and land that remains as the residence. Where the existing home is not demolished and only one unit is built, which becomes the owner's home, that is not carrying on an enterprise and so no GST will be payable.

A person registered for GST can claim all of the GST they pay on the construction costs of the residence they will be selling. They must also include GST in the selling price if it is sold within five years of the building being completed. If the property is sold after five years, GST is not included in the selling price, and if GST had been claimed on the construction costs this must be paid back to the ATO.

When it comes to selling a residential property it is very hard, in effect almost impossible, to require the purchaser to pay an extra 10 per cent on top of the selling price. This means the sale price for residential property includes GST.

The bad news is that you lose one-eleventh of your selling price in GST paid to the ATO; the good news is you will be able to claim the GST on the construction costs. As a result of paying the GST your capital gain will be reduced, and you won't pay as much income tax on the gain if the property is not your residence. Had you been registered for GST at the start a lot better tax result could have been achieved by having used the margin scheme.

Where no GST is included in the original purchase of a property, the seller can use the margin scheme (a way of working out how much GST must be paid on the sale of a property). For the margin scheme to apply, in addition to no GST having been included in the original purchase price of the property, the contract for the resale of the property must clearly show that the margin scheme is being used. This means if the ATO discovers you should have been registered for GST after the sale of the property, it is too late to use the margin scheme, as the sale contract would not have included the required clause.

Under the margin scheme, GST is payable on the difference between the original non–GST inclusive cost of the property and its selling price. The original cost of the property cannot include other purchase costs, such as stamp duty and legal fees. The selling price used must include any settlement adjustments contained in the sales contract. The GST payable will be one-eleventh of the difference between the purchase cost and the selling price.

The effect of not being registered for GST, and therefore of not being able to use the margin scheme, is demonstrated by the following example.

The consequences of not registering for GST

Jack and Jill purchase a home in 1996. They learn that due to a change in council regulations their property can be subdivided. They decide to build a unit on the vacant subdivided land instead of just selling it.

After the building is completed and landscaping done, the subdivided property is sold for $660 000. The ATO, from information supplied by the state land titles office, issues Jack and Jill with a GST assessment for $60 000. Because they can claim the GST of $20 000 included in the building costs of the new house, they end up with a net GST bill of $40 000.

If Jack and Jill had registered for GST and stipulated in the sale contract that the property was being sold subject to the margin scheme, the GST payable would have been less. If they had been aware that they were subject to GST and registered for it, Jack and Jill would have had a valuer apportion the cost of the property between the house and land it now stood on and the subdivided block. If the cost of the subdivided block was $220 000, and they had used the margin scheme, GST of only $40 000 would have been payable. The actual amount of GST payable by Jack and Jill would again have been reduced by the GST they had paid on the construction costs of the unit, so their net GST payable would have been $20 000. By being registered for GST and using the margin scheme, Jack and Jill would have saved $20 000 in GST.

Example 2: investing in commercial property

Investors who have recognised the benefits of investing in commercial properties, for both an income and a capital profit, have purchased everything from a corner shop to an office building. GST can be payable when a commercial rental property is owned and the annual rent exceeds the $75 000 registration threshold. When this occurs GST must be included in the rent charged, but the investor can also claim the GST they pay on such things as agent's fees, insurance and repairs.

No GST is payable on rent from domestic properties, as this is classed for GST purposes as input-taxed income. Under this category, no GST is charged on the income produced and no GST can be claimed on any costs associated with earning the income.

Income tax

Income tax for most people is a once a year thing. For those who prepare their own tax return, it is often regarded as a boring chore; for those who get it done for them, the appointment is regarded as being slightly less painful than a visit to the dentist. Many people treat tax with a lot of fear and loathing, which can lead to some irrational decisions being made. A number of times in my professional career, after showing a client how they can earn more from their investments, they have asked, 'Why would I want to do that? I'd end up paying more tax.'

Thankfully there is no income tax rate, apart from tax payable on excess super contributions, that results in someone paying more tax than they earn. The highest tax rate in Australia, including the Medicare levy, is 46.5 per cent. This means that when someone earns more money, they are at least 53.5 per cent better off. If this extra income can be earned without any effort, you have to ask yourself the question, 'Why wouldn't you?'

Many people concentrate only on the cost of something. I try to assess options on a cost-benefit basis. The activities that have the greatest net excess benefit, or the least net cost, tend to be the best options.

If people are aware of the income tax rules that directly affect them, they can organise their affairs in a more tax-effective way. This does not mean I expect you to become a tax expert, but it does mean that, by having a basic understanding of these various tax issues, you will avoid the tax traps and know the right questions to ask.

The first thing to understand about income tax is that the amount you pay depends on four things. These are:

- assessable income
- deductible expenses
- marginal tax rates
- tax offsets and rebates.

Assessable income

For most people it is obvious if they are receiving assessable income. As is often the case, however, income tax legislation, rather than providing a clear description, shrouds the concept in mystery and legalese.

This is how the relevant section of the income tax act defines assessable income:

6-1(1) Assessable income consists of ordinary income and statutory income.

6-1(2) Some ordinary income, and some statutory income, is exempt income.

6-1(3) Exempt income is not assessable income.

6-1(4) Some ordinary income, and some statutory income, is neither assessable income nor exempt income.

6-1(5) An amount of ordinary income or statutory income can have only one status (that is, assessable income, exempt income or non-assessable non-exempt income) in the hands of a particular entity.

To think that someone was actually paid to draft this! I'll explain each of these points overleaf.

Personal note

Since 1989 I have covered every federal budget, except one, for Melbourne's *The Age*. This meant flying to Canberra on a crisp, cold May morning, being locked in a room for about seven hours and poring over a stack of budget papers.

One reason for this lack of clarity in taxation legislation became clear to me when one budget was handed down in the early 1990s. A new taxation measure had been announced that did not make sense. When I asked one of the Treasury staff for help, his answer provided a rare insight into how tax law is drafted. He said, 'I only write this stuff; it is up to the tax office to interpret it'. To this day I'm not sure whether he was joking or he was deadly serious.

Ordinary income

In simple terms, ordinary income is something you receive regularly, such as salary, wages, rent and interest. Money received in one-off amounts tends to be capital receipts, such as the proceeds from the sale of an investment, or windfall gains, such as a lotto or lottery win. Windfall gains are not classed as assessable income and so are tax-free.

This tax-free status of gambling or prize winnings is different from the US, where these are taxed. In Australia the money a weekend punter wins at the races is not assessable. If, however, they put all of their energy and effort into gambling, including spending a great deal of time researching horses and racecourses, and they produced a net income from the gambling activities, they would be taxed on these winnings.

This also means that if you receive a gift of cash or an asset this is also not taxable. However, the person making the gift could be required to pay CGT on the asset if the gift is an asset that has increased in value since they bought it.

Statutory income

Statutory income is amounts you receive that the government has decided you must include as taxable income. This has been done in most cases to make the tax treatment of certain income more certain. The best example of statutory income is a capital gain you make on the sale of an investment.

Exempt income

Exempt income is anything the government has legislated as not being taxable. The most recent example of this is pension and lump sum payments received from a taxed super fund by someone aged 60 or more. Another example of exempt income is the 50 per cent small business active asset exemption that small business owners receive when they sell their business. This means after using the general 50 per cent discount and the active asset exemption only 25 per cent of the capital is assessable.

Income that is neither exempt nor assessable

A new category of income was introduced in 2003–04, which is income that is not assessable but is also not exempt (numbered 6-1(4) in the list on p. 65). This basically means no tax is payable on it, but it does not fit into any of the other classifications. An example of this income is when a person makes a capital gain on the sale of an active business asset, and they have owned the business continuously for 15 years. If they satisfy the small business CGT concession rules, the capital gain is not assessable, but it is also not classed as exempt income by tax laws. Unlike the 50 per cent active asset exempt income, this gain is not assessable due to the 15-year retirement small business concession, but it is not exempt income.

Income has only one status

The final part of the bewildering legal definition of income (numbered 6-1(5) in the ATO's list on p. 65) is there to protect taxpayers. It means that although you receive something that could be classed as both assessable income and statutory income, it can only be taxed once. It does not have to be included in two different sections of a tax return or in two different years.

What is included in assessable income?

For most people assessable income includes:

- salaries and wages
- allowances and benefits
- government pensions and benefits

- some superannuation pensions, depending on your age
- interest
- dividends
- distributions from trusts and partnerships, including managed investments
- net rental income
- capital gains
- foreign income
- net business income.

Whether a person is running a business will depend on the facts of the case. Where a business is not being operated, the income produced is not assessable. Where the facts of a case support that income comes from a hobby, it is not assessable, and the costs related to earning the income are not deductible.

Some of the indicators of a person having a hobby rather than operating a business, are where the activity is done on a part-time basis; the activity is not organised; no records are kept; no actions such as advertising are taken to maximise the amounts received; and the prime motivator for the activity is enjoyment and not the making of a profit.

Business losses

There are also tax rules designed to stop people reducing their taxable income through a non-commercial loss. To be able to claim a business loss against other income, you must satisfy one of the following tests:

- assessable income from the activity is at least $20 000
- a profit has been made in three out of the past five years (including the current year)

- real property or an interest in real property worth at least $500 000 is used in the business on a continuing basis
- other assets (such as plant and machinery) worth at least $100 000 are used in the business on a continuing basis.

Another area where losses can be made and used to decrease taxable income are rental property activities. In these cases, as long as the property does not have a private aspect, losses can be offset without any other tests applying. A rental activity can be regarded as being private or domestic in nature when it is rented for less than market value. In this situation it is not a rental property for investment purposes, and the loss cannot be used to reduce taxable income from other sources.

All of these types of assessable income accumulate to become a person's total assessable income. This concept is important to understand for wealth creation planning. When a capital gain is made, it is added on top of all other assessable income. By anticipating a capital gain a person can, by using a number of tax-planning strategies, reduce their assessable income and pay CGT at a lower marginal tax rate.

Deductible expenses

For an item to be classed as a deductible expense it must not only be a loss or outgoing incurred in producing or gaining assessable income, it must also have been necessarily incurred in gaining or producing the assessable income. There must be a connection between the amount spent and the income earned for an expense to be tax deductible, and it also must have been 'necessarily incurred'. By adding this second qualification, an expense that has been incurred but was not essential to earning the income is not deductible. An example of this would be a person who works in an office and decides to purchase a more comfortable chair to be used solely at work. As a chair was supplied by their employer, and it was not necessary for the employee to buy a more comfortable chair, the employee could not claim the cost of the chair against their employment income.

Even when there is a connection between an amount spent or incurred and income earned, there are three qualifiers or types of expenditure that can make it not tax deductible. These include items that are:

- of a capital, private or domestic nature
- incurred in gaining or producing exempt income
- not permitted as a tax deduction by something in the income tax laws.

Most people will not have expenses related to producing exempt income, and hopefully rarely have costs that are specifically banned from being tax deductible. This second group of expenses includes such things as penalties and fines.

Costs of a capital, private or domestic nature are encountered on almost a daily basis. Capital costs are the original purchase price of an item or asset. In most cases, the cost of something that will last longer than 12 months cannot be claimed in full in the year it is purchased. A good example of this for an individual is the cost of gaining a professional qualification. This cost is effectively regarded as a capital cost, being the ability to earn an income, and is not deductible. By contrast, the costs of maintaining a qualification — for example, by attending seminars and conferences — are deductible.

Capital costs can be claimed as a tax deduction if they are items of small value. For individuals, this is items that cost less than $300; for small businesses, it is currently items that cost less than $1000.

Whether an item is private or domestic in nature in most cases will be obvious. For example, you cannot claim a tax deduction for the cost of the gas and electricity used in your home. Since everyone must wear clothes, the cost of normal clothing is regarded as domestic or private in nature and is not tax deductible.

Some costs have a dual purpose, with some portion relating to earning income. The portion relating to earning an income is tax deductible, but the remaining portion is private and domestic in nature and so is not tax deductible. An example of this is motor vehicle costs. A tax deduction cannot be claimed for private travel in a car, such as private trips with your family or driving to and from work, but where a car is used in relation to income-earning activities, the costs will be deductible. (Refer to the section later in this chapter about claiming car expenses.)

"Stockings and guns are allowed, but you can only claim a portion of your car. How often was it used to get away?"

Employment-related deductions

Currently a person can claim up to $300 of employment-related deductions without having the necessary evidence to support the claim. Where a claim is made under the kilometre method for car expenses (discussed later in the chapter), this is not included in the $300 limit.

There are some other exceptions to needing receipts. Where your employer requires you to wear protective clothing or a uniform, a claim for up to $150 a year for cleaning can be made without having to produce receipts.

A person who must do work at home, and has a separate room to work in, can claim a portion of their actual lighting and heating costs. They can also claim a tax deduction based on the number of hours the home office is used in a year multiplied by 26 cents. Where work is done in a room shared with other people, such as a corner of a family room, no claim can be made for lighting or heating costs.

Where allowances are paid for such things as travel and overtime meal allowances, a claim can be made equal to the allowance received without having to produce receipts.

For other expenses, there still needs to be a connection between the expense and the employment income, and you also need to be able to produce evidence to support the claim. These include:

- interstate and overseas business travel
- training and seminars
- mobile phone and home telephone costs
- technical journals, periodicals and books
- professional association and union subscriptions
- self-education when there is a connection to employment and the possibility of an increased income from the study.

Professional note

In Australia we have a taxation system based on self-assessment. This means the income tax returns lodged by individuals are regarded as being correct until they are audited by the ATO. It is a common fallacy that something is tax deductible because the ATO has not rejected the amount claimed. Many times during my professional career, after informing the client that something was not tax deductible, they said that it must be, because one of their work colleagues had been deducting it years. There are many things that people claim as tax deductions that they shouldn't, and they will not have a problem until they are audited by the tax office.

Interest and dividend deductions

Costs associated with earning interest and dividends can be claimed as a tax deduction. This includes subscriptions to investment magazines, professional fees for reviewing a portfolio, interest on loans taken out to fund the investment, and bank fees and charges associated with a bank account or loans used for investment purposes.

A cost that would be classed as a capital expenditure is brokers' fees associated with the purchase of shares. These costs are added to the purchase cost of the shares and can be used to reduce any future capital gain or increase any capital loss.

An extremely large cost that many Australians pay, and in some cases are not even aware of, are the entry commissions charged by financial planners when they prepare a plan that results in investments being purchased. These commissions are a capital cost and not tax-deductible.

Distributions from trusts and partnerships, including managed funds

Tax-deductible costs in this area are similar to those related to interest and dividends. They include interest on the funds borrowed to purchase the investment; professional fees related to reviewing the performance of investments; and administration and platform management fees.

Rental deductions

Rental deductions include all costs associated with the renting activities of a property, including interest, rates and agent's fees. For a more detailed discussion, refer to chapter 9.

Foreign income deductions

Costs associated with earning foreign income can be deducted. They include interest on loans to make the investment and other costs associated with the investment.

Business deductions

Business deductions are far too numerous and complicated to go into in this book. For those interested in this area please refer to my book *Tax for Small Business* (Wrightbooks, 2008). The same principles that apply to apportioning costs between private and business purposes also apply to a business. If in doubt you should seek professional advice.

How much tax you pay

Subtracting all the tax-deductible expenses from all the assessable income produces the amount of an individual's taxable income. The amount of tax payable will depend on their total taxable income and what tax offsets they are eligible for. For example, where fully franked dividend income has been received, the actual tax payable on share earnings will be decreased by the total amount of franking credits received. Tax offsets are discussed later in this chapter.

Marginal tax rates

Marginal rates of tax are the different levels of tax payable on different levels of taxable income earned (as shown in table 4.1). The higher the income you earn the higher the tax rate payable.

Table 4.1: marginal tax rates for resident adults, 2010–11*

Annual taxable income ($)	Tax on income ($)		Tax rate on excess above lower threshold (%)
0–6000	0	plus	0
6001–37 000	0	plus	15
37 001–80 000	4 650	plus	30
80 001–180 000	17 550	plus	37
180 001 plus	54 550	plus	45

*Excludes Medicare levy.

Tax residency

The residency of a person dictates how their income is taxed. But the residency tests used by the tax office are different from Australian citizenship tests. Under income tax law, whether a person is a resident is decided by a series of tests.

The first of those tests requires a person to have resided in Australia continuously for a period of 183 days during the financial year.

The next, and more important, test is the domicile test, which requires a person to establish their normal place of abode. The application of this test can result in someone who has been in Australia for more than 183 days being classed as a non-resident for tax purposes, and someone who has been overseas for longer than 183 days classed as a resident. Normal place of abode is effectively where a person's home is. That is why a backpacker who spends two years travelling and working around Australia, but has their home overseas, would not be classed as a resident. Conversely, someone who takes up an overseas job for three years, but retains their home in Australia, would be classed as a resident for tax purposes. The marginal tax rates for non-resident adults are shown in table 4.2.

Table 4.2: marginal tax rates for non-resident adults, 2010–11

Annual taxable income ($)	Tax on income ($)		Tax rate on excess above lower threshold (%)
0–37 000	0	plus	29
37 001–80 000	4 650	plus	30
80 001–180 000	17 550	plus	37
180 001 plus	54 550	plus	45

Note: Non-residents do not pay Medicare levy.

Marginal tax rates for minors

Where a person aged less than 18 earns income other than salaries and wages, such as distributions from family trusts and investment income resulting from a gift, punitive rates of tax apply, as shown in table 4.3.

As minors are also entitled to the low income tax offset, the actual amount of income that they can earn before paying tax in 2010–11 is about $3333.

Table 4.3: tax rates for income earned by minors, 2010–11*

Other income ($)	Tax rates
0–416	Nil
417–1307	Nil + 66% of the excess above $416
Over 1307	45% of the total amount of income that is not excepted income

*Excludes Medicare levy.

Medicare levy

In addition to paying income tax, a resident adult must also, depending on their total taxable income, pay a Medicare levy of 1.5 per cent. For the 2009–10 year, a single person whose income was less than $18 488 did not have to pay the Medicare levy; a couple who earned less than $31 196 was also exempt from paying the Medicare levy. For a family, the threshold increases by $2865 for each dependent student or child on top of the couple's threshold for payment.

The thresholds at which no Medicare levy is payable increase each year. The increase for the 2010–11 year will be announced when the federal budget is handed down in May 2011.

An additional Medicare levy surcharge of 1 per cent is payable by people whose income exceeds a threshold if they do not have private health insurance, or if they have private health insurance with too large an excess. For singles, the surcharge threshold is taxable income of greater than $77 000; for couples it is $154 000, and for families with more than one child the threshold increases by $1500 for each dependent student or child.

Tax offsets and rebates

Individuals can also claim a number of tax offsets that reduce the actual amount of income tax payable. The main tax offsets are described here.

Low income tax offset

All Australians are entitled to low income tax offset (LITO) if their taxable income is below two thresholds. The maximum rebate of tax available is $1500 for people with income below a threshold of $30 000. This decreases once a person's taxable income exceeds $30 000 at a rate of 4 cents for each extra dollar. LITO cannot be claimed once a person's taxable income exceeds the second threshold of $67 500.

Senior Australian tax offset

The senior Australian tax offset is available to people who are of Centrelink age pension age. The rates are shown in table 4.4.

Table 4.4: senior Australian tax offset rates, 2010–11

	Maximum offset ($)	Shadeout threshold ($)*	Income at which offset cuts out ($)
Single	2230	30685	48525
Couple (each)	1602	26680	39496
Couple separated due to illness (each)	2040	29600	45920

*The rebate reduces by 12.5 cents for each $1 of taxable income above the shadeout threshold.

Dependent spouse tax offset

Where one member of a couple earns little income, and where no family tax benefit part A or B is received, a tax offset can be claimed by the other member of a couple.

For the 2009–10 year, the maximum offset was $2243. Where a spouse's adjusted assessable income exceeds $282 in the financial year relating to the spouse, the offset decreases by $1 in every four that exceeds the threshold. This offset increases each year when the federal budget is handed down. We will not know the 2010–11 offset until after the 2011 federal budget. The offset cuts out once a spouse's adjusted taxable income reaches $9254. Adjusted taxable income for most people is made up of a spouse's normal taxable income plus fringe benefits, tax-free pensions and reportable super contributions (contributions made by an employer and salary sacrifice contributions).

Mature age worker tax offset

A person is eligible for the mature age worker tax offset (MATO) if they are aged over 55 at the end of the financial year; are an Australian resident for income tax purposes; and have earned income from working below a particular threshold.

For someone with a net income from working of up to $10 000, the MATO is 5 per cent of that income. The maximum amount of MATO receivable is $500, up to a net income from working of $53 000. Once a person's net income from working exceeds $53 000, the offset decreases by 5 cents for each dollar in excess. Once a person earns $63 000 or more in income from working, they are not eligible for the MATO.

Net income from working includes salaries and wages, personal services income, assessable income from the business carried on by the tax payer, payments from farm management deposits, reportable fringe benefits, reportable superannuation contributions, and other income, such as commissions, director's fees and bonuses. The total of this income is decreased by the allowable tax deductions related to its production.

Medical expense tax offset

A tax offset of 20 per cent of net medical expenses in excess of $2000 in a financial year is available. This threshold stood at $1200 for many years and was then increased to $1500, and only recently raised to the current threshold of $2000. The net medical expenses are those costs actually paid after deducting Medicare and health fund refunds. They are the net medical costs for not only the taxpayer, but also the net costs for their spouse and dependents.

Medical expenses include payments to doctors, hospitals, dentists, physiotherapists and other health professionals. Other payments relating to a medical condition, such as pharmaceuticals, medical equipment and other items prescribed by a doctor, are also included.

Payments to low- and high-care facilities, such as hospitals and nursing homes, can also qualify as eligible medical expenses. These include:

- basic daily care fees
- income-tested daily care fees
- extra service fees
- accommodation charge
- periodic accommodation bond payments
- retention amount deducted each year from accommodation bonds.

Payments for hospital cover and those relating to elective surgery, such as cosmetic surgery, are not counted. In addition, the cost of travel and accommodation that directly relates to medical treatment is not included.

Superannuation pension offset

Where a person receives a taxable superannuation pension and is aged under 60, they receive a tax offset equal to 15 per cent of the taxable pension received and included in assessable income.

Maximising your tax deduction for cars

A tax deduction can be claimed when a motor vehicle is used as a part of employment or income-earning activities. Driving from home to a place of employment and return is not classed as tax-deductible travel. Travel from a person's home to a customer's or supplier's place of business and then on to work, and travel from work to a customer's or supplier's place of business then home, is classed as tax-deductible travel.

Where travel from home to a place of employment is in a vehicle that carries bulky tools, equipment or goods, this can be classed as tax-deductible travel. An example of this would be a salesperson who must carry a wide selection of goods and promotional material with them at all times.

Once you have established that you can claim motor vehicle expenses, you have a choice of using one of the following four methods to calculate the amount you can claim:

- the kilometre method
- the 12 per cent of original value method

- the one-third of actual cost method
- the logbook method.

The kilometre method

Under this method, the tax deduction is calculated by multiplying the business kilometres travelled, up to a maximum of 5000 a year, by a cents per kilometre rate. Although no documentation has to be kept to prove the number of kilometres claimed, you must be able to reasonably show how you arrived at the number of tax-deductible kilometres driven.

The rate paid varies depending on the engine size of the vehicle. The rates for the 2009–10 year are shown in table 4.5. The ATO, depending on changes to the running costs of motor vehicles, issues new rates each year. The changes tend to be announced just before the end of the financial year they will relate to.

Table 4.5: rates paid for business travel when the calculation uses the kilometre method

Engine size of car	Cents per kilometre rate
Up to 1600 cc	63
1600 cc to 2600 cc	74
Over 2600 cc	75

These rates apply to conventional cars; for rotary cars and motorbikes, different engine sizes or rates apply. These can be found at <www.ato.gov.au>.

Where two or more cars are owned in a year, and 5000 or more kilometres are travelled in each of the cars, a maximum claim for each vehicle can be made using this method. The thing to remember is that you must be able to reasonably show how much tax-deductible travel is done in each car.

The 12 per cent of original cost method

Where it can be shown a motor vehicle travels more than 5000 tax-deductible kilometres a year, a claim can be made equal to 12 per cent of the original cost of the vehicle, up to the annual depreciation cost limit. For the 2010–11 year this limit is $57466. For example, a car that cost $30000 would produce an annual tax deduction of $3600. This depreciation cost limit increases each year, but by only very small amounts. Visit the ATO website for the latest cost limit.

The one-third of actual running costs method

Another method that can be used where a motor vehicle travels more than 5000 tax-deductible kilometres a year is the one-third of total running costs method. Under this method the tax deduction is calculated by dividing all costs associated with a car by three. Running costs include fuel, repairs, registration, insurance, motor association subscriptions, road and bridge tolls, lease payments, interest on loans and hire purchase contracts, and depreciation.

The logbook method

As I have mentioned, the things that require the greatest work and sacrifice often produce the best results. Maximising a claim for motor vehicle expenses is no exception. Under the logbook method, the tax-deductible use of a motor vehicle is calculated by keeping a logbook for 12 weeks.

At the end of the 12-week period the number of tax-deductible kilometres driven is divided by the total kilometres driven over the period, to arrive at the percentage of tax-deductible use of the vehicle. A tax deduction is calculated by multiplying the total running costs of the vehicle for the year by the tax-deductible percentage. Where a person's travel does not change greatly, this percentage can be used for up to five years, after which time a new logbook must be kept, once again for 12 weeks. The old logbook must be retained for the five years that it is used and for five years after the last year a claim based on it is made.

A logbook must show the day each journey began and ended, the odometer reading at the start and end of the journey, the length of the journey in kilometres and the reason for the journey. In addition, the logbook must show when the logbook period begins and ends, the odometer readings at the beginning and end of the logbook period, the total number of kilometres travelled during the logbook period, the number of kilometres travelled on business and the percentage of business kilometres within the total kilometres travelled.

Personal note

Over the years I have had to keep several logbooks. To make sure that I did not miss any travel I got into the habit of writing information in the logbook every time a got in the car. I wrote down the date, the kilometre reading at the start of the trip and the purpose of the trip. By doing this every time, even for private and domestic travel, I automatically had the closing kilometre reading for the previous trip.

In addition, when I needed to use the car for tax-deductible reasons, I combined the travel with a private purpose. For example, if I had to go to a stationery supplier to get something for work, I also purchased things I needed for home. This strategy works as long as the private travel is incidental to the business travel. It would not be acceptable to class a trip that involved a detour of more than a kilometre for a private purpose as entirely business related.

The fringe benefit tax method

There is one final way of ensuring the running costs for a motor vehicle are tax effective when no tax-deductible kilometres are driven. This method uses the motor vehicle provisions of the fringe benefits tax (FBT) system and is available to people whose employers allow them to package their salary.

FBT is payable on motor vehicle benefits in two ways. The first uses an actual cost method, and FBT is calculated and paid according to the private use of the vehicle. The second is the statutory method, where the FBT is calculated and paid based according to the number of kilometres the vehicle travels in a year and its purchase cost.

The FBT method works best for people who are paying tax at the top marginal rate; when the private vehicle is financed through a lease; when the vehicle is driven more than 25 000 kilometres a year; and when the car costs less than approximately $57 000. Before choosing this method to fund the running costs of a vehicle, it is important to get professional advice. In some circumstances using the FBT system can result in more tax being paid.

Capital gains tax

Strictly speaking there is no such thing as capital gains tax (CGT). Instead, what we have is a system that sets out how a taxable capital gain is calculated. This assessable gain is then included as taxable income and income tax is paid on it. Profits made on the sale of assets purchased before 20 September 1985, when CGT was introduced, are not included as assessable income. Profits made on the sale of assets bought after that date are included as assessable income.

The amount of gain that must be included in assessable income will depend on how long the asset has been owned. For assets held for less than 12 months, the full amount of the gain must be included in assessable income. If you hold the assets for 12 months or more you will be entitled to a discount on the capital gains.

For assets purchased up to 21 September 1999 a person can choose to use either the indexation method or the general 50 per cent discount method. For assets purchased after 21 September 1999, only the general 50 per cent discount method can be used. Under the indexation method, the gain made is reduced by the inflation that applied from when the item was purchased up until 21 September 1999. In most cases the general 50 per cent discount provides the greater benefit.

These discounts are available only to assets owned by individuals and trusts; they are not available when an asset is owned by a company. As a general rule, investment assets are best owned by individuals or trusts to ensure that, for assets held for longer than 12 months, tax is paid on no more than 50 per cent of the gain.

Under income tax law, the relevant date of purchasing or selling an asset is not the date on which settlement takes place, but the date of the contract. This is not a problem for most investments, except for property. In this case settlement can take place any time from 60 to 120 days after a sale contract has been signed. This means that where a sale note to sell a property is signed in one tax year, and settlement takes place in the following year, the relevant date for CGT is the earlier tax year. For sales that are conditional upon the purchaser getting finance or selling another property, the relevant sale date is still the date the sale note was signed.

When calculating the capital gain made on the sale of a property, all associated costs can be used to reduce the profit. These costs include the purchase costs, such as stamp duty and legal fees, the costs associated with maintaining the property, and the selling costs, including the real estate agent's sales commission.

For rental properties, most holding costs will have been claimed against the rental income. Holding costs include council rates, interest on a loan taken out to buy the property, water rates, repairs and maintenance, and the cost of any improvements or additions made to the property. Once all costs have been taken into account, and provided the property was owned for more than 12 months, tax will be payable on half of the capital gain remaining.

Properties that have been used for private purposes, such as a holiday home, will have a greater number of holding costs that can be used to decrease the capital gain.

Tax planning tip

If an offer is received in the last weeks of June for an investment property, and you do not want to jeopardise the sale, it makes sense to accept the offer after 30 June and sign the sale note then.

The same principle applies to shares that will produce a capital gain. If the price of a share will not be adversely affected, it makes sense to not place the shares with your broker for sale until after the end of the financial year. Where a capital loss will be made, it makes sense to sell the shares before 30 June so that the loss can offset against gains made in that year.

Capital gains tax exemptions

Very few assets are not subject to CGT. The two exceptions are a person's home and motor vehicles. A number of rules and calculation methods apply to the CGT exemption of an individual's main residence. Before they can be considered the property must first qualify as a main residence.

The factors taken into account for a property to qualify as a main residence include:

- the length of time the property has been owned and whether your family live there
- whether it is used as your mailing address
- whether you have all of your personal possessions there.

In the end, one of the prime determining factors is your intention in occupying the property, which must be borne out by the facts.

There is no minimum time limit that must be met for a property to be classed as a main residence. This can mean that, where someone buys a property to live in and after only a short time shifts interstate for personal or employment reasons, the property will qualify for the CGT exemption as long as they do not buy another residence.

One time period does apply to the main residence exemption: it requires the owner to move into the property as soon as practicable after its purchase. This can mean where there is a valid reason supported by facts, such as illness or other unforeseen circumstances, the exemption will still apply if there is a delay between moving in and purchasing the property.

An area limit and two time limits also apply to the main residence exemption when it comes to land. The area limit means the CGT residence exemption applies only to a home on no more than two hectares.

For vacant land you have up to four years to class it as your main residence, as long as during that time you construct a home and move into it as soon as practicable after its completion. The second time limit requires that the home remain your residence for at least three months after moving in.

This means a person can have one main residence that they live in while building a new home on land they have purchased. As long as the new home is constructed within the four years, and they live in the new home for at least three months, they will receive the main residence CGT exemption for their original home and the new property.

There is another situation where the main residence exemption will apply to two properties for up to six months. This will occur when:

- you purchase a new property
- the original property was used as the main residence for a continuous period of three months over the previous 12 months of ownership
- you don't rent or produce income from the property during those 12 months

- you sell the original residence within six months of purchasing the new one.

A person can only claim the residence exemption for one property at a time. If for some reason the owners of a home leave it and live elsewhere, as long as they don't purchase another residence and don't rent out the property, the residence exemption will apply indefinitely.

Properties used for a dual purpose

In four situations a property can have two uses. Examples of this are as follows:

1   A property is first used as a home then used to produce rental income when a new home is purchased.

2   A property is originally used as a home and then a portion of it is used to produce income, such as when the owners start a home-based business.

3   A property is originally purchased for rental purposes and then becomes a home.

4   A property is purchased as a home and the owners move out, do not purchase another home, and rent out the property.

Two methods can be used to calculate how much CGT is payable when a property is used as both a residence and to produce income. The first method, the valuation method, calculates the taxable gain based on the increase in the value of the property after its use has changed. The second method calculates the taxable gain based on days of ownership.

Where a property starts out as a residence and then becomes a rental property after 20 August 1996, such as occurred in numbers 1 and 4 above, the valuation method must be used.

In this situation the taxpayer is deemed to have acquired the property at its market value when the change of use occurs.

Under the valuation method, when the property is disposed of CGT is payable on the amount that the net sale proceeds received exceed the market value of the property when it started producing income. It is important if you are in this situation to engage a valuer who understands that you need the valuation for CGT purposes.

Tax planning tip

In what can only be described as an interpretation by the ATO that maximises tax revenue, if a property becomes a rental property and is sold in less than 12 months, the taxpayer cannot get the benefit of the 50 per cent general discount. This will be the case even if the property had been owned for many years while being used as a residence.

This interpretation of the law by the ATO has to my knowledge not been tested yet. Unless you are prepared for the cost and trouble of challenging the ATO, and you have a property that was once your home that is now being rented, you should wait at least 12 months before selling the property to ensure you can benefit from the 50 per cent general discount.

The days of ownership method is used to calculate the capital gain when a property is first used to produce assessable income and then becomes a residence, as outlined in number 3 in the list on p. 90, or when a property starts to be used as a residence and is then rented while the owners are absent, as outlined in number 4 in the list on p. 90.

Under this method, the number of days the property was used for rental purposes, expressed as a percentage of the total days of ownership, becomes assessable for CGT purposes.

An example of this is a property rented for five years, which is then used as a residence for five years, and then sold. Half of any gain made will be assessable for CGT purposes.

Where a residence is rented out while the owners do not own another residence, the residence exemption applies for a maximum of six years. Once the six years are exceeded, unless the owners cease renting and move back into the property, the CGT clock starts ticking. An example of this would be a couple who own their home for four years; they both move overseas to take up employment and rent their home as soon as they leave; and they then sell the property after having been away for 11 years. For this couple two-thirds of the capital gain will be eligible for the residence exemption (because they have the residence exemption for six of the 11 years of renting), and only one-third will be caught for CGT. After receiving the 50 per cent general exemption, they will pay tax on only 16.7 per cent of the gain.

CGT when you subdivide

The capital gains tax exemption for a residence is limited to a house on no more than two hectares. A house on land measuring less than two hectares can still result in a CGT liability. This occurs when the original block purchased is subdivided. Where the original home is retained and the vacant block is sold, CGT will in most cases be payable. If, instead, a new home is built on the vacant block, and the original home sold, there should be no capital gains tax payable.

Where residential property is subdivided, the original home continues to be lived in, and either the vacant subdivided land is sold, or built on and sold, the original value of the land must be split. This can best be calculated by engaging a registered valuer.

How CGT is paid

CGT is not a separate tax but is included as part of a person's assessable income, as the following example will show.

Simon has owned a holiday house for many years and he has decided to sell it. He is employed full-time and has taxable income for the year before the capital gain of $100 000. The calculation is shown in table 4.6.

Table 4.6: an example of how CGT is paid after the sale of a holiday house

	$	$
Selling value of rental property		410 000
Less		
Agent's selling commission	12 000	
Adjustment for rates, etc.	1 000	
Total sale costs		13 000
Net sale proceeds received		397 000
Less purchase and holding costs		
Original cost	120 000	
Stamp duty, etc.	4 000	
Extension	40 000	
Interest on loan over time property owned	23 000	
Council rates over time property owned	10 000	
Total costs		197 000
Capital gain		200 000
Less 50% general discount		100 000
Taxable gain		100 000

The taxable gain of $100 000 will be added to Simon's other assessable income of $100 000 making a total for taxable income of $200 000. Tax will be paid on the gain at 37 per cent on the first $80 000 and at 45 per cent on $20 000, resulting in total tax payable of $38 600. In addition, Simon will pay 1.5 per cent Medicare levy on the full $100 000.

If Simon had been married and the property was jointly owned with his wife, he would have paid tax on $50 000 at 37 per cent. The remaining $50 000 would be taxed in his wife's hands, and if she was not working, no tax will be payable on the first $6000: tax on the next $31 000 would be payable at 15 per cent: and the $13 000 remaining would be taxed at 30 per cent, making her total tax payable $27 050.

Capital gains and death

When a person dies the tax payable on their assets varies according to what the asset is and when it was purchased. Certain assets, such as a person's home and their super-annuation, receive special tax treatment. Assets that had been purchased by the deceased before 20 September 1985 also receive special treatment for capital gains purposes.

The proceeds of a deceased's superannuation, when paid to their dependants, is not taxable. When it is paid to non-dependants, tax is paid at 16.5 per cent (including the Medicare levy) on taxed benefits. A dependant for super-annuation purposes includes a person's spouse or any of their children or other people that they have an interdependency relationship with. In most cases this will mean children under 18 will be classed as dependants.

Capital gains tax payable on the other assets of a deceased person will also depend on whether they are sold by the executor of the estate, or sold at some later date by the person who inherits them.

If the executor of the estate sells the assets, the relevant purchase date, to decide how much tax will be payable, is the date the deceased purchased the asset. Any assets purchased before September 1985 will be tax-free, while anything purchased after then will have the capital gain taxed by the estate.

The exception to this will be if the executor or the person inheriting the property sells the deceased person's home within two years. In this case no tax is payable on the gain.

Other assets owned by the deceased for more than 12 months will have tax paid on half of the gain. Assets owned for less than 12 months will have tax paid on the full gain.

When the ownership of assets passes directly to a beneficiary of the estate the capital gains tax treatment also differs according to when the assets were purchased. Assets purchased by the deceased before September 1985 are taken to have been purchased by the beneficiary at their market value at the deceased's date of the death. When a person receives assets from the estate of someone who died before 19 September 1985, they are regarded as having inherited a pre-CGT asset.

If the deceased purchased the asset after 19 September 1985 the cost for the person inheriting the asset will be the same as it was for the person who died and originally bought it.

The CGT issues are simpler when assets are owned by a discretionary trust instead of by the person who died. In this situation no change in ownership occurs as a result of the death, as the assets in the trust are not regarded as assets of the deceased.

Conclusion

At this point in developing a strategy to fund your retirement you will know what your goals are; what you own and what you owe; how much money you are earning after tax; how much money you need to meet your living expenses; and have at least a basic understanding of superannuation, and income tax regulation and laws. The next thing to consider is the best way to organise your investments.

CHAPTER 5

The different investment vehicles

I have already likened most people's financial lives to a long journey: just as it is important to make sure a car will get you where you want to go, it is also important to make sure the investment vehicle you choose is the right one to fund your retirement.

There is no doubt that the premier vehicle for funding your retirement is superannuation, because it offers so many tax advantages. However, if you plan to retire early, before you can access your superannuation, other investment vehicles or ownership structures must be used.

It is a fact of investing life that the younger you are the simpler your investment structures need to be. As a person gets older, and their investments increase, the number of possible investment structures and their complexity increases.

The different ways investments can be owned are:

- as an individual
- jointly with one other person or a number of other people
- through a family discretionary trust
- through a unit trust

- through a company
- through a superannuation fund.

Each of these ownership structures offers various benefits and disadvantages when it comes to income tax. The following section explains each of the structures and its advantages and disadvantages.

Individually held investments

Holding your own investments as an individual is by far the simplest way to own investments and is the way everyone starts off. In many cases this investment would have taken the form of a savings account while you were at primary school. When you are single, this is probably the best structure to own investments that will be held outside superannuation.

The disadvantage of owning investments as an individual is that all the income earned is taxable at your marginal tax rate. If a large capital gain or other investment income is earned, tax may have to be paid at one of the higher marginal tax rates.

For a couple where one person isn't working, there can be an advantage to having investments in that person's name. This will ensure that any investment income earned will be taxed at lower marginal tax rates.

Where interest and other costs exceed an investment's income, it makes sense to have the investment in the name of the person who is earning more income, because the investment loss will generate the bigger tax refund. The disadvantage is that when the investment is sold, and a large capital gain is made, tax will be paid at the higher marginal tax rates of the bigger earner.

Jointly held investments

The most common example of jointly held investments is when they are held in the joint names of a couple. When both members of the couple are on the same taxable incomes, with the income being split equally, the risk of paying tax at a high marginal tax rate on all the income earned can be reduced. This is especially true when capital gains are made.

Where an investment is negatively geared, joint ownership does reduce some of the tax benefit where one person is on a high income, but it does mean that at least half of any capital gain made will be taxed at the lower marginal tax rate of the other member of the couple.

Family discretionary trusts

There is a general principle that you have to spend money to make money. When it comes to tax structures, the principle is that the more complicated and costly the structure, the more tax effective it is likely to be. Owning investments as an individual or jointly is very simple and uncomplicated. A family discretionary family trust, on the other hand, is complicated and can be expensive to set up and maintain, but it is the most flexible and tax-effective structure available.

The cost of setting up a trust depends on who the trustee is. Where an individual is the trustee, the set-up cost will be about $700. This will cover the cost of drawing up the trust deed and paying the government fees.

In some cases people choose to have a company act as trustee for the trust. This can be useful where a trust is being used to operate a business and the owners want some protection for their personal assets, but it is not so useful as a structure to hold investments. When a company acts as trustee, the set-up costs increase to about $1600.

Taxation

A family discretionary trust is the most tax-effective structure for owning income-producing investments. This is because the income can be distributed among the family members to ensure tax is paid at the lowest possible rate.

Family discretionary trusts have been around for many years, and when Australia had death taxes, these trusts were used primarily to reduce death duties. Since then, they have become a very popular vehicle through which to own investments and operate a business.

Unlike when investments are owned either individually or jointly, and the owners must pay tax on the income and capital gains made, the income of a discretionary family trust can be distributed to the members of that family in whatever proportion the trustee decides.

The amount of tax saved by distributing to family members is maximised the more children there are, and if the children are 18 or older and have not commenced working full-time. This is because non-working children under 18 can only receive about $3300 before they have to pay tax. Income distributed above this level will be taxed at the top marginal tax rate at least.

Distribution of income

When a trustee distributes income to a beneficiary of a trust, the trust does not have to physically pay them the money. The distribution is often made by the trustee drawing up a minute that states how much of that year's net investment income is distributed to each of the beneficiaries. This distribution is recorded in the books of the trust, and the beneficiaries are taxed on that income even though they don't receive it, as an amount owed to each. As money is actually paid to, or on behalf of, each beneficiary the amount of money owed to them by the trust reduces.

There is a risk attached to distributing income to children. When no amounts are actually paid to them, or the distributions to children are not recorded properly, large loans can build up that the children are entitled to. In the event of a family dispute, major financial problems can be created if the children demand payment of the debt owed to them by the trust.

To ensure that these loans do not become too large, costs relating to the children, such as education fees, holidays, tax on income distributed to them and car expenses, should be paid by the trust instead of the parents. By doing this, the loan owing to each of the children will not keep increasing and there may even be a situation where the children owe the trust money.

If trust income is distributed to individuals, the 50 per cent general capital gains tax exemption (for assets bought after September 1985 and held for more than 12 months) applies when investments are sold for a profit. If a capital gain is distributed to a company, the 50 per cent discount is lost.

Unit trusts

Unit trusts are not used very often and they tend to be used when an investment is owned by non-associated investors, such as happens when unrelated people invest in a property.

In this case the unit trust buys the property and units in the trust are issued. The income and capital gains from the investments are distributed to the unitholders in the proportion they own the units.

Unit trusts are often used when a large number of people come together to buy one or several investments. Listed property trusts and managed share funds are examples of unit trusts.

Every trust must have a trustee that conducts its day-to-day business. The cost of setting up a unit trust will be determined by whether individuals are going to be trustees or a company. Depending on who you use to set up the unit trust, and how complicated the trust deed is, it can cost from $400 to more than $1000 if individuals are the trustees. Where a company will act as the trustee, the set-up cost increases by about $900, making a total set-up cost of between $1300 and $1900.

The treatment of capital gains in a unit trust is the same as for a discretionary family trust.

Companies

Companies are possibly the worst structure for owning investments. This is because when capital gains are made on the sale of investments a company does not receive the 50 per cent general discount that an individual would get.

The main advantage of using a company structure for holding investments is that tax can be paid on investment income at the 30 per cent company tax rate. If the shareholders of the company do not take accumulated profits in the company, the after-tax profits can be distributed at a later date when the shareholders have retired and have low levels of taxable income.

Companies are reasonably costly to set up and maintain and, because they do not get the 50 per cent general capital gains tax exemption, they do not offer much benefit for most investors.

Superannuation

From a legal perspective superannuation funds are a form of trust. In this case, super contributions are made on behalf of or by members, and the trustees of the superannuation fund invest the contributions. Just like the other tax structures, the type of super fund a person uses can change over their investing life.

Functions of a super fund

To better understand how superannuation funds work, it is important to understand the four main functions they perform. They are:

- compliance and accounting
- administration
- provision of insurance cover
- investment of the funds.

Compliance and accounting

The compliance and accounting function ensures a super fund complies with all the superannuation and tax laws, and keeps accurate records of each member's superannuation benefits. The accounting function keeps track of all transactions of the fund, such as contributions, income, taxation and withdrawals. The accounting function is also responsible for producing reports that are correct, easy to understand and issued in a timely way.

Administration

For large superannuation funds the administration function is often the most labour intensive. The administration area is responsible for answering members' questions, processing requests from members, including commencing pensions or paying out benefits, and issuing the various reports that keep members up to date.

Provision of insurance cover

Most superannuation funds offer various types of insurance, including life insurance, disability insurance and income protection insurance. The types of insurance a member needs, and the amount of cover required, depend on the individual's personal circumstances. (See chapter 7 on how to reduce risk.)

The cost of cover can vary widely between funds. In some cases, where a member requires a high level of insurance cover, the cost of insurance can rule out of consideration a fund that has low fees and charges. In some cases, a more expensive super fund can be more cost effective because of lower insurance costs.

Investment of the funds

The investment of the funds can make or break a super fund. In some cases, the investment of money in a superannuation fund is handled internally by its own staff. In other cases, external fund managers handle all the fund's investment, or investment can be managed by a combination of both internal and external professionals.

The more investment choice a super fund offers members—for example, of different fund managers and different sorts of investments, such as direct shares—the better. This does not mean the member has to use all the options available, or have an intimate knowledge of investment markets and fund managers, but by having a wide variety of different investments to choose from, members get the chance to maximise their superannuation.

One way in which a person can maximise their investment funds for retirement is to be aware of the administration costs and investment returns of their super fund.

What the individual can control in super

The only three things that a person has control over when it comes to maximising the amount of superannuation they will have at retirement are:

- the amount of personal contributions, both concessional and non-concessional, that they make
- the administration fees charged by their super fund
- how much income the super fund's investments earn.

The other two things that affect how much super a person accumulates are income tax on super fund contributions and earnings, and the superannuation guarantee contributions made by employers. The member cannot control either of these, unless they are prepared to find a new employer that contributes more than is required under the superannuation guarantee system.

It is important, therefore, if you want to maximise your assets for retirement, that you are aware of the three things you can control when it comes to your superannuation.

The level of contributions you make personally will depend upon how much of your income you can divert into superannuation. The amount of administration fees you are charged, which for some people includes commissions paid to financial advisers, and your investment returns from the fund can both be controlled by making an informed choice of what super fund and investment option best suit you.

Like most things it would be wrong to concentrate just on the cost or the investment returns when choosing a superannuation fund. There is not much point in switching to a super fund that has extremely low administration fees, but below industry standard investment performance. It also does not make sense to choose a super fund that has above-average investment performance, but with administration fees set so high that they result in underperformance as a whole.

Types of super fund

Currently there are three main types of superannuation funds. They are:

- industry superannuation funds
- commercial or public offer super funds
- self managed super funds.

As a result of the Cooper review into superannuation, which reported in mid 2010, and the acceptance by the Gillard Labor government of most of its recommendations, at some point in the future a fourth choice will be added, called MySuper. It will be a default option for employees who do not choose a super fund. We'll consider MySuper first in the following discussion, because there is widespread political support for this account and it seems likely to become available in the next few years.

What super fund is best for you?

People often have different types of superannuation funds over their working life. When someone is starting off and they do not have a great deal in superannuation, some of the cheaper no-frills options can be best. As a person gets older and accumulates more money in superannuation, a more expensive but flexible superannuation fund may be chosen.

The best way I know of comparing the four options available is to stress the point that a superannuation fund is an investment vehicle. Just like the choices a person faces when selecting the make and model of car they own, the defining features of the different types of superannuation funds are very similar. It is therefore important to make sure the super fund you choose will get you to retirement in the most efficient way.

MySuper

MySuper accounts will be offered by both industry and commercial superannuation funds. They will be similar to the base model offered by car manufacturers, such as a Falcon, Commodore or Corolla. They won't have many options or features, the driver won't need a lot of help in driving this vehicle; it will be inexpensive to maintain; and it will get you to your destination.

As MySuper accounts will be offered widely, and because each provider of a MySuper account must clearly detail all of the costs and performance of the member's account, it should be relatively easy to determine which MySuper account is best for you. This will most likely be the best model for someone who is just starting the superannuation journey.

The main features of a MySuper account that will affect members are:

- a single diversified investment strategy that will suit most members who choose the default option
- restrictions on unnecessary or excessive fees
- a ban on commissions and entry fees being charged to members
- restrictions on the payment of performance fees to fund managers
- limitation of exit fees to cost recovery
- the offer of life and total permanent disability insurance on an opt-out basis.

As part of the introduction of MySuper, the Gillard Labor government wants a review to be conducted of the default superannuation funds named in modern awards. The aim of this review will be to have MySuper accounts become the main super funds that can be used as default funds.

It is my hope that default funds will not apply to you, because default funds are super funds that employers and the industrial awards specify that an employee will belong to when they do not make an active choice of fund and do not return a completed standard choice form to their employer. As you are reading this book, I assume that you care enough about your retirement investments to complete and return the super choice form.

The government intends to have MySuper legislation passed during the 2011 calendar year so that all super funds, except self managed super funds (SMSFs), will be allowed to offer MySuper products from 1 July 2013.

Industry superannuation funds

Industry super funds have in many cases seen the greatest development and improvement over recent years. These funds were originally like the base model offered by the major car manufacturers, offering few options and, in some cases, providing limited reliability or driving pleasure.

In some cases industry funds have improved their levels of service and the options they offer members. This is a bit like what has happened with some Asian car manufacturers, which started off with cars that were regarded as cheap and nasty, but now produce good-quality vehicles.

Commercial funds

Commercial funds are often a lot more expensive than other funds, but they appeal to people who want a bit more performance from their super. These funds often offer a great many more choices and options when it comes to investing, but this increased choice often comes at the cost of the member requiring professional help, which adds to the cost of the fund.

If the right model has been chosen, and the advice received comes from a professional adviser who is not driven by commissions, an individual choosing a commercial super fund can experience better performance despite the extra costs.

Self managed super funds

Generally known as SMSFs, self managed super funds are the four-wheel drive model of superannuation funds. They offer almost unlimited options, and the flexibility to go to where ever you want when it comes to investing. They'll get you where you want to go when it comes to superannuation and retirement.

Due to the number of options they have, and because they really are a specialist vehicle, they require more professional help in driving and maintaining. If they are used without the right advice, money may be saved, but they can end up being used incorrectly and cost the member dearly.

SMSFs mainly suit superannuation fund members who have large superannuation balances of $300 000 or more and want to have greater control over their own financial and superannuation destiny. SMSFs have grown in popularity to the point where the funds held by SMSFs make them the largest type of super fund in Australia today. SMSFs are discussed in more detail in the following section.

What is an SMSF?

For a super fund to be classed as an SMSF it must meet the following conditions:

- there must be no more than four members
- all members must be trustees as individuals or as directors of a trustee company
- no member can be an employee of another member, unless they are a relative of that member
- trustees cannot be paid in cash or kind for any duties they perform as trustees.

To understand how an SMSF operates, the following is an explanation of how the four main functions of the super fund are handled by an SMSF.

Compliance and accounting

The responsibility for the compliance and accounting function in an SMSF is placed firmly on the shoulders of the fund's trustees. People who have the skills and time can perform most of the required tasks themselves, while others, who lack the skills, time or inclination, can have this function carried out by their accountants or a specialist SMSF service provider.

Administration

It is in the administration function of a super fund that an SMSF can really excel. As long as the trustee members of an SMSF do not contravene any of the relevant laws and regulations, they can do almost anything whenever they want.

This is another case of where the duties and jobs associated with this function can be performed by the trustees themselves or shared with a service provider or accountant.

Members of the other types of super funds who receive substandard service, such as lengthy delays in requests being actioned, often just have to put up with it, due to the level of bureaucracy associated with these funds. If a member of an SMSF is on the receiving end of substandard service, the responsibility is their own.

Insurance cover

This function is one where most SMSFs are at a disadvantage. Large super funds can get access to group insurance cover that is a lot cheaper than can be obtained by individual members of an SMSF.

Where insurance cover is required, and insurance premiums for an SMSF are prohibitive, SMSF members can have a second super account through an industry or commercial fund so they can take out insurance.

Investment of the funds

The type and number of investments that the trustee and members of an SMSF can have are limited only by the relevant rules and regulations. The almost unlimited choice can be a problem for the trustees of an SMSF. However, when the trustees understand the various investment rules and regulations, and when in doubt consult with their professional adviser, this should not be a problem.

An SMSF is really the only choice when a person wants to have the greatest say in their own superannuation destiny, and if they want to invest in the following direct investments through their super:

- residential property
- commercial property
- works of art
- collectables
- first mortgages with solicitors
- unlisted investments, such as private companies and unit trusts
- joint ventures in an investment with a member or related party.

The high cost of getting it wrong with an SMSF

In all there are seven rules that trustees of an SMSF must follow and are tested against to allow them to run an SMSF. The rules are as follows:

1 The fund must meet the sole purpose test of the superannuation funds only being allowed to be used for retirement purposes.

2 An investment strategy has to be recorded in writing.

3 Loans and financial assistance may not be given to members.

4 In-house assets, such as investments purchased from members, cannot exceed 5 per cent of market value of the fund.

5 Assets may not be purchased from related parties, who include members and their relatives, except in limited cases.

6 Investments must be commercial and at arms length.

7 Extremely limited borrowing is allowed.

If an SMSF fails even one of these rules the tax office imposes a number of penalties. Depending on the severity of the offence, civil penalties of fines up to $220 000, or imprisonment for up to five years, can be imposed. The main punitive weapon the tax office has, which it can impose without reference to a court of law, is the declaration that the super fund is a non-complying fund. When a fund is classed as non-complying, 46.5 per cent of the fund's assets can be taken in tax penalties and all future income of the fund is taxed at 46.5 per cent. Given the severity of the penalties, it does not make commercial sense for anyone to knowingly breach any of the rules.

For a greater understanding of the rules relating to SMSFs refer to my book *Self Managed Super Funds* (Wrightbooks, 2009).

Conclusion

When a person is in the early stages of accumulating their superannuation the new MySuper account should be the best option. As their super balance increases, and they want to have a greater say in the management of their super funds, an industry or a commercial super fund may suit them. However, when a person wants the greatest say in their own superannuation destiny and to invest in a wide range of direct investments not available through other types of super fund, an SMSF is really the only choice.

CHAPTER 6

Strategies for funding your retirement

By this stage in thinking about funding for your retirement you should:

- have a written list of your short-, medium- and long-term financial and life goals
- worked out what you want and need to earn in retirement
- know what you own and how much you owe
- have calculated how much money you're making after tax, and what your domestic expenditure budget is
- know what excess income is available for wealth creation
- have a basic understanding of superannuation and Centrelink rules
- understand how the income tax and capital gains tax rules work
- have worked out what super fund is best for you and have an understanding of the other types of investment structures that can be used to save for retirement.

The next stage in funding retirement is putting in place plans and strategies that ensure your investing capacity is used instead of being spent on discretionary items and lifestyle. Up until this point, the book has all been about working out what you want and where you are now.

This chapter deals with the various strategies to help you put into place an action plan. It is designed to help you stop just thinking about investment and start doing something. Because people go through various financial stages in their life I have listed the strategies in the order they apply.

THE 'JESSE JAMES' RETIREMENT PLAN FOR PROCRASTINATORS

Source: <www.CartoonStock.com>.

Stages of life and preparation for retirement

Many of the strategies can be applied at any stage in a person's financial life. One of the most important strategies — salary sacrifice — applies at every stage. This is because although it is best to start salary sacrificing as soon as possible in your working life, it can still produce great financial benefits at any stage of a person's financial life.

The major life stages are:

- stage 1 — the single years when most of your money is spent on having fun
- stage 2 — you are starting to earn more income and thinking about buying a home or investing

- stage 3—the age of family and mortgage commitments
- stage 4—the years before retirement, often a time of fewer commitments and some spare cash that can be invested
- stage 5—just before age 65, just before or just after retirement, when you aim to maximise your assets for retirement.

Professional note

Some of the strategies suggested apply at every stage of life. When I'm preparing wealth creation strategies for clients I continually check back to what the cash consequences are of each strategy. Some strategies, because they are using tax laws to the client's benefit, result in a small after-tax cash flow cost.

When deciding on your own strategies, or when assessing strategies that have been prepared for you, you must make sure you always have enough cash to meet your desired domestic expenditure budget, plus some extra as a safety margin.

Stage 1

In life stage 1, you are young and single and most of the cash generated from working is spent on having a good time. In this life stage, tomorrow and retirement goals seem too far away to think about seriously.

Salary sacrificing into super

As the name of this strategy implies, some sacrifice is required for the salary sacrificing into super strategy to work. The sacrifice here is forgoing a small amount of pre-tax salary or wages by diverting this money into superannuation as a concessional (pre-tax) contribution. Because the amount sacrificed is made before tax is deducted from your salary, the drop in your disposable income is relatively minor.

Table 6.1 sets out how much extra superannuation a person will have contributed over a period of one to 40 years after a $20 per week salary sacrifice, and what it costs. The results shown are presented on an annual basis and do not take account of the improved financial performance as a result of contributions being made at least quarterly. The higher the marginal rate of tax a person pays, the smaller the reduction in spending power and the greater the overall benefit. However, even for someone paying tax at the lowest rate, there is a small benefit.

The earlier this type of strategy is implemented the greater the overall increase in superannuation investments. A weekly salary sacrifice amount of $20 results in a cash flow loss after tax of just $16.70 a week at the lowest tax rate, and $13.70 at the tax rate most people pay. Over a 40-year period, the pain of this sacrifice comes at the gain of an extra $136 810 in super. To put this into perspective: if you forgo about three Big Mac meals a week and divert the money into super, this extra superannuation will pay you about an extra $156 a week in retirement.

The disadvantage of salary sacrifice is that you have to wait until you reach retirement to get a benefit. An advantage of this strategy is that, depending on what your employer allows, the amount sacrificed can be increased as your earning capacity increases and stopped altogether if you experience financial hardship.

Table 6.1: the growth in super fund balance over 1–40 years after $20 per week salary sacrifice

Marginal tax rate* (%)	Change	Weekly change ($)	Year 1 ($)	Year 10 ($)	Balance Year 20 ($)	Year 30 ($)	Year 40 ($)
	Increase in value of super	17.00	884	11 652	32 518	69 887	136 810
16.5	Reduction in after-tax spending	16.70	868	11 442	31 931	68 625	134 337
31.5	Reduction in after-tax spending	13.70	712	9 385	26 193	56 292	110 194
38.5	Reduction in after-tax spending	12.30	640	8 435	23 542	50 595	99 044
46.5	Reduction in after-tax spending	10.70	556	7 329	20 454	43 959	86 052

*This is the applicable marginal rate of tax plus Medicare levy of 1.5%.

Note: Results shown reflect an annual rate of return of 6 per cent on funds invested.

Investing in insurance bonds

If you know you have an ability to invest, and you would like a tax-effective investment that imposes a certain level of discipline, you should consider investing in one of the modern insurance bonds.

The old form of insurance bonds tended to be sold by insurance salesmen. The investor had to make do with whatever earning rate the insurance company decided to pay, and in many cases the person selling the bond made more money than the investor.

Modern insurance bonds are based on what has become known as a wrap account or investment administration platform. These insurance bonds allow a person to invest their funds with a number of different fund managers and investment funds. The insurance company offering this type of insurance bond charges an administration fee.

Instead of accepting whatever earning rate the insurance company decides to pay you, modern insurance bonds give you a level of control that allows you to choose from among a number of products and fund managers. If an insurance bond is kept for 10 years, the proceeds are tax-free.

An insurance bond also allows a person to invest regular amounts over the whole 10-year period of the bond, which imposes a discipline that diverts funds from a bank account before you have a chance to spend it.

If access to the investment is required before the 10 years are up, there are still tax benefits. Income earned on a bond cashed in up to eight years after commencing is taxed at the investor's marginal tax rate, reduced by a 30 per cent tax offset. This means only 15 per cent tax is paid on the bond's earnings by someone on the top tax rate of 46.5 per cent.

If the bond is cashed in the ninth year, one-third of the income is treated as exempt income and two-thirds is treated as normal income. If a bond is cashed in the tenth year, two-thirds of the income is treated as exempt and one-third as taxable. In both cases, the taxable income from the bond receives the 30 per cent tax offset.

Controlling and consolidating debt

One of the biggest temptations at this stage of life is credit cards. Provided you exercise financial discipline, a credit card can be a great way of having more money to work for you if the interest-free period is used. When you don't exercise discipline, a credit card can become an ever-tightening financial noose around your neck.

Credit card debt that has become a problem requires drastic action. Sometimes it can even come to cutting up all of your credit cards or at least not carrying them around with you — excess credit card usage is often the result of impulse buying. This habit could come from browsing clothes shops and not being able to resist a bargain; checking out what movies are out on DVD and not being able to resist a two-for-one offer; or browsing the web and ending up on eBay, where you buy the Norwegian combination staghorn bottle opener and engine degreaser that you could not live without.

If you don't want to give up carrying your credit cards around, you need to break the bad habits. If possible, find a way to get directly to the shop you really *need* to go to, and not go anywhere near clothing and DVD stores.

For some people, overspending on credit cards or signing up for mobile phone deals that cost more than you can afford can result in a debt that cannot be repaid and a default is recorded. This may not seem a huge problem when you are young, but a bad credit rating can come back and haunt you. It could be when you are trying to get a loan for a car, or when you are in stage 2 of your financial life and want to borrow to buy a home.

Diverting cash into a high interest earning account

Diverting cash into a high interest earning account is a strategy that can be used at any age, but it makes a huge difference when used when you are young. Today, when we can get cash from a bank account via a debit card, we need discipline and planning to ensure we don't just spend all of our available cash.

Instead of saving money in jam jars, this strategy revolves around setting up a high interest online account. Set up a periodic transfer to the online account from the cheque account or other bank account that your employment income is paid into. Ideally you should transfer an amount that leaves just enough to fund your normal day-to-day living expenses in your everyday account. The money in the high interest online account can be used to fund large annual bills, such as insurance and motor vehicle registration, and any extra cash not required to meet your domestic expenditure budget can be allocated to other wealth creation strategies.

Stage 2

You are starting to earn more income. You might have a partner now, and you're starting to think about putting money aside to buy a house or start investing.

Salary packaging

Being able to package your salary varies depending on employers. Some employers are not flexible and do not allow their employees to sacrifice their salary as a superannuation contribution. Others will not only allow employees to salary sacrifice into super, they also offer other packaging options, such as paying for a fully maintained motor vehicle.

For some not-for-profit organisations, such as hospitals and charities, salary packaging can even include paying up to about $8000 in before-tax mortgage repayments or up to $8000 in entertainment costs. If you work for one of these organisations it makes a great deal of sense to maximise your before-tax salary packaging options.

If the only salary packaging option, apart from super-annuation, is to have a fully maintained motor vehicle, think carefully before taking up this option. This is because motor vehicle salary packaging is regulated through the fringe benefits tax (FBT) system.

What normally happens under this packaging option is that a motor vehicle is purchased and financed through a novated lease. Novated leases are taken out in the name of the person who owns the car, but the employer is shown as being responsible for making the lease payments out of pre-tax salary. The total running costs for the vehicle, including the lease repayments, are deducted from a person's salary. In addition, however, the salary is further reduced by the FBT payable by the employer.

In most cases the FBT that applies is calculated using what is known as the statutory method, which is briefly explained in chapter 4. This salary packaging option works best for motor vehicles that cost less than $40 000, are driven more than 25 000 kilometres a year, and the salary sacrificed would have tax paid on it at the 45 per cent marginal tax rate, plus the Medicare levy of 1.5 per cent.

Before committing to a motor vehicle salary packaging offer, seek professional advice to ensure you will actually be better off as a result of funding the cost of your car this way.

Salary sacrificing into super

If you found that you could not sacrifice some of your salary or wage into super in stage 1 it is not too late to start. Diverting $50 a week into super, as table 6.2 shows, results in a reduction in after-tax spending a week of between $34.25 and $26.75. The benefit is an increase in your super of $2210 a year, which over 30 years results in an extra almost $175 000 to help fund your retirement.

Again, the only downside to salary sacrifice is that you cannot access the income diverted into super until you meet a condition of release (see chapter 3).

Diverting cash into a high interest account for a house deposit

Diverting cash into a high interest account for a house deposit is a similar strategy to the one used in stage 1, but it is done with the goal of saving enough for a deposit on a home.

If two of you are saving, it makes sense to put the high interest account into the name of the person who earns the lower income. If one member of a couple is earning $45 000 a year, and the other is on $80 000, it makes sense to put the high interest account into the first person's name. This is because all the interest earned will be taxed at 31.5 per cent instead of one half being taxed at 38.5 per cent if the account was in joint names.

Table 6.2: the growth in super fund balance over 1–40 years after $50 per week salary sacrifice

Marginal tax rate* (%)	Change	Weekly change ($)	Balance					
			Year 1 ($)	Year 10 ($)	Year 20 ($)	Year 30 ($)	Year 40 ($)
	Increase in value of super	42.50	2210	29130	81296	174719	342024
31.5	Reduction in after-tax spending	34.25	1781	23475	65515	140803	275631
38.5	Reduction in after-tax spending	30.75	1599	21076	58820	126414	247464
46.5	Reduction in after-tax spending	26.75	1391	18334	51169	109970	215274

*This is the applicable marginal rate of tax plus Medicare levy of 1.5%.

Note: Results shown reflect an annual rate of return of 6 per cent on funds invested.

Making a non-concessional super contribution of at least $1000

Since 1 July 2004 people on lower incomes have been encouraged to make after-tax non-concessional super contributions through the Commonwealth Government's co-contribution scheme. In this scheme, the government paid into the member's super account up to 150 per cent of a person's non-concessional contribution, up to a limit of $1500 a year. The maximum co-contribution now stands at 100 per cent, and the maximum that can be paid is $1000.

The maximum co-contribution available in the 2010–11 financial year is for people with incomes up to $31 920. The co-contribution reduces by 33.34 cents for every $10 by which a person's income exceeds the low threshold, until the high threshold of $61 920 is reached, when no co-contribution is payable. Where a person qualifies for only $1 of co-contribution, the minimum amount paid is $20. Someone with a total income of $50 000 who made a non-concessional contribution of $1000 will be eligible for a co-contribution of $397.

The income assessed for payment of the co-contribution is a person's total assessable income, plus reportable fringe benefits and reportable employer super contributions (which includes salary sacrifice contributions), minus any allowable business deductions. By allowing business deductions to reduce the total income this effectively means only the net business income is counted.

The co-contribution is available only to people who are working, as 10 per cent or more of a person's total income must come from either employment or carrying on a business.

The co-contribution is payable where a person is less than 71 years of age at the end of an income tax year.

This strategy is particularly applicable for a couple where one member is the main income earner, and the second person works part-time and so has income below the low threshold. For someone in this situation a non-concessional contribution of $1000 a year, with the super fund earning 6 per cent a year in investment income, this would result in an increase in superannuation of $79 995 over 20 years.

Paying off your HECS or HELP debt in lump sums

Where you have undertaken tertiary education to obtain a qualification, you will more than likely have a debt relating to the cost of that education. This HECS or HELP debt can be paid off in several ways. The most common way is by your employer making deductions through a payroll system to fund the required minimum repayment each year.

Once a person's taxable income exceeds a low threshold an increasing percentage of their taxable income is used to repay a HECS or HELP debt. For the 2010–11 financial year the repayment thresholds and rates are as shown in table 6.3 (overleaf).

HECS or HELP repayment income (HRI) is the income figure used to calculate the HECS or HELP repayment amount. It is made up of a person's total taxable income, plus any investment losses, such as from a negatively geared property, reportable fringe benefits and reportable super contributions. Any exempt foreign employment income is also included in HRI.

After a person's income tax return is lodged each year, their HECS or HELP debt increases each year at a rate that reflects inflation, and decreases each year by the amount paid according to the minimum repayment schedule.

Table 6.3: minimum thresholds and rates of repayment for HECS or HELP debt, 2010–11

HECS repayment income level ($)	Repayment rate (percentage of HECS repayment income)
Below 44 912	0.0
44 912–50 028	4.0
50 029–55 143	4.5
55 144–58 041	5.0
58 042–62 390	5.5
62 391–67 570	6.0
67 571–71 126	6.5
71 127–78 273	7.0
78 274–83 407	7.5
83 408 plus	8.0

If you have the capacity to invest, you can repay a HECS or HELP debt more quickly by making lump sum repayments. Lump sum payments of more than $500 result in a 10 per cent bonus. For example, a $1000 lump sum payment reduces a HECS or HELP by $1100. This is like receiving a 10 per cent tax-free return on your investment.

Moving overseas and becoming a non-resident for income tax purposes

I'm not advocating that you leave Australia and stop being a resident just to obtain a financial benefit. But if you are planning on working overseas for an extended period, and so will not be classed as a resident for Australian income tax purposes, a financial benefit can be obtained where you have a HECS or HELP debt.

While working overseas as a tax non-resident, any HECS or HELP debt you have will increase in line with inflation, but the income earned overseas will not be counted for the annual repayment of the HECS or HELP debt. By making regular lump sum repayments while you are overseas you will receive the lump sum payment bonus; the inflation charge will apply to a smaller debt; and the debt will be paid off more quickly.

Investing in a negatively geared property

In the introduction to this book I stated that wealth creation is mainly about diverting income into investments away from supporting a lifestyle. An effective and popular way of doing this is to purchase a rental property using borrowings.

In this situation the rental income is often exceeded by the interest and other costs associated with the property. The costs include real estate agents' fees, rates, and repairs and maintenance. If the property purchased was constructed after 1985, in addition to claiming a tax deduction for the depreciation of fixtures and fittings, a deduction can also be claimed for 2.5 per cent of the construction costs of the building.

Because the costs of the property will exceed the rent produced, income must be diverted to fund the shortfall. The actual cash cost to the investor is reduced by deducting the tax property loss from other income earned, such as salaries and wages. This tax benefit can be received during the year if an application is made to the ATO to vary the PAYG tax withheld by your employer. You can also receive the benefit as a lump sum tax refund after the end of the financial year after lodging your tax return.

If you do not need the extra cash to fund the negatively geared property for living expenses, it makes sense, in the absence of using other wealth creation cash-diverting strategies, to wait for the lump sum tax refund. This is because this lump sum can be used to fund a non-concessional (after-tax) super contribution or for some other wealth creation purpose.

The rental income produced from residential property as a percentage of its value in most cases is very low when compared with the return from other investments. Traditionally most of the investment return from a residential property comes from capital growth. Care therefore must be taken when purchasing a property to ensure that all the capital gain potential of the property is maximised as is discussed in chapter 9.

Committing to investing in a property using borrowed funds has many risks. If the affordability of the investment is based on producing rental income for 52 weeks of the year, any period when tenants are either in default or the property is not rented, can put a severe financial strain on a person's cash flow.

For a more complete discussion of how investing in property works, refer to chapter 9 about the pitfalls and benefits of property investing.

Investing in the sharemarket

Another way to divert income from being spent is investing in the sharemarket. Dollar cost averaging and margin lending are two strategies for this investment.

Dollar cost averaging works if you commit to investing a regular amount into either direct shares or managed share funds. This strategy involves a person investing a set amount either monthly or quarterly. The secret of the strategy is to ensure the amount is invested regularly, no matter what the sharemarket is doing.

In times of great market volatility, when the values of shares are regularly moving up and down, investing regular amounts makes a great deal of sense. That means sometimes you'll pay a higher price for shares, while at other times the price will be lower; but, over the long term, the cost of the investment in the sharemarket will have been averaged. It also means the investor can build a substantial investment in this area over a period of time rather than trying to accumulate a lump sum amount to invest at once.

Care needs to be taken in choosing direct shares or managed share funds to invest in, to make sure a reasonable dividend income is produced and the chances of capital growth are maximised. Unless you are experienced in evaluating shares and/or managed share funds you should seek professional advice.

Where you have a lump sum to begin this investment strategy, such as a tax refund produced from other investing activities, you can consider increasing the amount invested by borrowing funds through a margin lending facility.

Margin lending works on the basis that the investor uses shares they already own as security for the facility or they have a lump sum in cash to invest in shares. The financial institution providing the finance advances funds to the investor up to a stated percentage of the value of the shares offered as security and being purchased. By using a margin lending facility an investor can increase the amount invested in the sharemarket. However, this comes with the risk of the investor being forced to sell their shares, often at a low price, to reduce the amount borrowed from the financial institution. This can happen if there is a major drop in the value of shares, as happened in 2008 when the global financial crisis hit. Under margin lending facilities, if the value of the shares securing the loan decreases to a certain level the lender can demand the repayment of some of the principal of the loan. If the investor does not have the cash to make this repayment, shares must be sold.

One way of ensuring that the risk of being forced to sell the investments is minimised is to limit the amount borrowed to no more than 50 per cent of the cash invested. For example, if the investment starts with $5000 in cash, only $2500 is borrowed using the margin facility. If $1000 a month is regularly invested, the margin lending should be limited to $500 a month. In these cases, as the borrowed funds make up no more than 35 per cent of the original amount invested, the chance of a margin call is greatly reduced. Table 6.4 and table 6.5 (on p. 134) show the effect of how dollar cost averaging and using margin lending would work over a 30-year period using two different scenarios.

In scenario 1, $1000 a month in cash and $500 a month via margin lending are invested over 30 years. In scenario 2, the cash investment and borrowing cease after year 10.

For both scenarios I have used an annual growth in the share investment of 5 per cent and an annual dividend yield of 3 per cent. From a historical point of view, the average annual return, including both income and capital growth for the All Ordinaries Index from 1900 to 2009, was 13.6 per cent.

Table 6.4: scenario 1— the effects over 30 years of investing $1000 a month in cash and $500 a month via margin lending for 30 years

	Year 1 ($)	Year 2 ($)	Year 10 ($)	Year 20 ($)	Year 24 ($)	Year 25 ($)	Year 29 ($)	Year 30 ($)
Share investment								
Opening balance		7 500	182 965	524 433	715 033	768 785	1 012 045	1 080 647
Cash invested	5 000	12 000	12 000	12 000	12 000	12 000	12 000	12 000
Margin loan	2 500	6 000	6 000	6 000	6 000	6 000	6 000	6 000
Growth at 5%		375	9 148	26 222	35 752	38 439	50 602	54 032
Closing balance	7 500	25 875	210 113	568 654	768 785	825 224	1 080 647	1 152 680
Margin loan								
Opening balance		2 725	51 709	81 036	62 391	52 825	−13 365	−38 245
Borrowing	2 500	6 000	6 000	6 000	6 000	6 000	6 000	6 000
Interest at 9%	225	515	4 924	7 563	5 885	5 024	−518	−1 762
Less share income 3%	225	225	5 489	15 733	21 451	23 064	30 361	32 419
Closing balance*	2 725	9 015	57 144	78 866	52 825	40 786	−38 245	−66 426
Borrowing as percentage of security value		34.84	27.20	13.87	6.87	4.94		

*Negative loan balance represents amount saved.

Table 6.5: scenario 2 — the effects over 30 years of investing $1000 a month in cash and $500 a month via margin lending for 10 years

	Year 1 ($)	Year 2 ($)	Year 10 ($)	Year 20 ($)	Year 24 ($)	Year 25 ($)	Year 29 ($)	Year 30 ($)
Share investment								
Opening balance		7500	182965	325954	396200	416010	505662	530945
Cash invested	5000	12000	12000	0	0	0	0	0
Margin loan	2500	6000	6000	0	0	0	0	0
Growth at 5%		375	9148	16298	19810	20800	25283	26547
Closing balance	7500	25875	210113	342252	416010	436810	530945	557493
Margin loan								
Opening balance		2725	51709	29835	-4584	-16549	-77259	-96142
Borrowing	2500	6000	6000	0	0	0	0	0
Interest at 9%	225	515	4924	2955	-79	-677	-3713	-4657
Less share income 3%	225	225	5489	9779	11886	12480	15170	15928
Closing balance*	2725	9015	57144	23012	-16549	-29707	-96142	-116727
Borrowing as percentage of security value		34.84	27.20	6.72				

*Negative loan balance represents amount saved.

In both scenarios I have used the share dividend income generated to pay off the margin loan. The dividend yield is calculated at 3 per cent of the opening value of the shares each year after taking account of a 5 per cent growth in value. The actual performance of the Australian sharemarket is much more volatile, as was demonstrated in the 1980s, when four of the 10 years produced negative results, one of which was as high as –39.9 per cent.

For calculation purposes, an annual 5 per cent growth rate over a 30-year period is not over optimistic. The long-term average return over any 10-year period since 1900 has not been less than 8.81 per cent, which was for the 10 years ending in 2003. In fact, after the biggest single drop in 2008, when the All Ordinaries dropped in value by 40.4 per cent, the 10-year average return was 9.35 per cent.

In scenario 1, dividend income pays off the margin lending loan by year 8 and in scenario two the loan is paid off by year 23. After each of these loans has been paid off I have assumed that the income has been reinvested at 5 per cent per year return.

This investment strategy particularly suits someone who wants to retire before they meet a condition of release to gain access to their superannuation. Care must be taken as, due to market volatility, extra cash may sometimes need to be invested to ensure a margin call is avoided. There may also be years where the dividend income generated must be supplemented with other cash to ensure that the margin loan does not become too large.

Before implementing this strategy, you should seek professional advice. This strategy is based upon a continuing income stream, so you should also take out income protection and life insurance.

Stage 3

This is a time when you have lots of commitments, which tend to come from having a family and a mortgage. The demands on your finances are the greatest now, and unless you are earning an above-average salary, things can be very tight financially and there may not seem to be much left for investing.

Salary sacrificing into super

Although this is a time in your life when your investing capacity may be significantly reduced by the financial demands of having a family, the after-tax impact of salary sacrificing is not that great, even on an amount of $100 per week (see table 6.6). Even if this strategy is used only for 20 years it can mean an extra $160 000 in superannuation, which translates to at least $150 extra per week income tax-free when you retire.

Investing in an insurance education bond

If you plan to have children, or have very young children who you would like to go to a private secondary school, this strategy is a tax-effective way of investing for their education, particularly using modern insurance bonds, which give you much more flexibility. These are described fully under the Stage 1 heading in this chapter.

This strategy also allows you to divert income away from the household so it can be used for wealth creation. It can be combined with other strategies that produce a tax refund, which can then be used as the initial deposit.

Table 6.6: the growth in super fund balance over 1–30 years after $100 per week salary sacrifice

Marginal tax rate* (%)	Change	Weekly effect ($)	Balance			
			Year 1 ($)	Year 10 ($)	Year 20 ($)	Year 30 ($)
	Increase in value of super	85.00	4420	58 259	162 592	349 437
31.5	Reduction in after-tax spending	68.50	3562	46 950	131 030	281 605
38.5	Reduction in after-tax spending	61.50	3198	42 152	117 640	252 828
46.5	Reduction in after-tax spending	53.50	2782	36 669	102 338	219 940

*This is the applicable marginal rate of tax plus Medicare levy of 1.5%.

Note: Results shown reflect an annual rate of return of 6 per cent on funds invested.

An insurance education bond can be started with as little as $2000 upfront and a $200-a-month savings plan. Table 6.7 shows that this type of investment will produce a tax-free lump sum of almost $33 500 after 10 years.

Table 6.7: earnings for an education insurance bond over 10 years

	Year 1 ($)	Year 2 ($)	Year 4 ($)	Year 6 ($)	Year 8 ($)	Year 9 ($)	Year 10 ($)
Opening balance	2 000	4 500	9 881	15 814	22 355	25 873	29 566
Amount invested	2 400	2 400	2 400	2 400	2 400	2 400	2 401
Income earned at 5%	100	225	494	791	1 118	1 294	1 478
Closing balance	4 500	7 125	12 775	19 005	25 873	29 566	33 446

If a person's financial situation changes, the regular investment amounts can be stopped, and the investment left in place to accumulate with earnings. In the event of a financial emergency, the funds could be accessed with there still being some tax benefits received, as was explained in the discussion of the Stage 1 investment strategies. Before commencing an investment like this, you should get professional advice from a fee for service adviser.

Consolidating your debts

There can come a time in people's lives when, in addition to a mortgage for their home, they have accumulated other debts, including personal loans and amounts owing on credit cards. It is not unusual for the interest rate on a personal loan to be 14 per cent per year and on the credit card debt, more than 20 per cent. If the mortgage has been in existence for some time, the amount owing may have reduced considerably from the originally borrowings. Where a person has been in regular employment, a combination of the repayments on the mortgage and an increase in the value of the home can create increased borrowing equity in the home. This equity can be used to refinance and pay out the high interest debts and consolidate everything into the mortgage loan, which is likely to be at a much lower interest rate.

Table 6.8 shows how debt consolidation works for someone who has an existing home loan, a personal loan for a car, and a large credit card debt they find hard to pay off.

Table 6.8: how debt consolidation can produce additional disposable income for investment

	Original balance ($)	Balance now ($)	Monthly payment ($)
Value of home	300 000	400 000	
Original home loan at 8% P&I* after 10 years	200 000	161 000	1 544
Personal loan at 14% for 5 years after 2 years	20 000	15 000	465
Credit card debt at 20%		20 000	400
Total monthly repayments			2 409
New home loan at 8% P&I over 15 years		196 000	1 873
Salary sacrifice			300
Extra earnings for investing other purposes			236

*Principal and interest.

Using the original home loan to pay off $35000 in their other debts, or taking out a new loan for $196000, can increase disposable income, and generate extra cash flow for investing of $536 a month. Using $300 of this additional cash flow to increase or start salary sacrifice into super would achieve a monthly increase in super of $438 if the person is on the 30 per cent tax rate, and $488 at the 37 per cent tax rate. Taking into account the 15 per cent contributions tax, and an earning rate of 6 per cent for the super fund, after 15 years a person on the 30 per cent tax rate would have increased their super by almost $104000; at the 37 per cent tax rate, they would have increased their super balance by almost $116000.

If $200 of the extra cash produced were used to increase the home loan repayment to $2073 a month, the home loan would be paid off in 12 and a half years instead of 15 years.

For this strategy to work, a person needs to prepare a detailed domestic expenditure budget and, if impulse buying resulting in excessive credit card use is identified as a problem, all but one of the cards should be cut up and it should be left at home.

Consolidating your superannuation

A person who has worked for several employers over their working life can end up with several super accounts in different funds. Some of those super funds may even be the old style of commercial fund that pays commissions and so has very high administration fees.

In this situation, review all the super funds, and work out which has the best combination of low fees and insurance premiums, and high returns. Roll all the other super accounts into this one. Super funds are often only too happy to help you roll over money from other super funds. If you are unsure about which of your super funds is the best, you should seek professional advice.

Splitting superannuation with a spouse

Under the current super laws a person can split their super with a spouse who is under 65 and not retired. Up to 85 per cent of their yearly super contributions, made by their employer (including salary sacrifice contributions) or as self-employed super contributions, can be split.

There are three reasons why this can be a powerful strategy for people. The first relates to the fact that a person must meet a condition of release to gain access to their super. This means if one partner is working, and they are under 65, they must either retire or resign from an employer to gain access to their super.

The second reason is that each partner, if they have not reached age 60, has access to a tax-free lump sum payment from their super which is currently set at $160 000 when they meet a condition of release. For many couples, if one has not been working or has been working part-time because they have been looking after children and running the home, the other tends to have nearly all the superannuation.

Super splitting with a spouse can mean the amount accessible as a tax-free payment is doubled (each receiving $160 000 tax-free). If the working spouse wants to continue working for as long as possible, the non-working spouse will still have access to their superannuation once they have met a condition of release.

The third reason is based on the assumption that the Gillard Labor government will pass promised legislation to retain the $50 000 maximum contribution per year for people aged 50 and over who have less than $500000 in superannuation. Super splitting with a spouse can ensure one partner keeps their superannuation below the $500000 level, while still maximising their ability to make super contributions and boosting their partner's super.

Stage 4

Stage 4 is the stage before retirement, or when people have stayed single or not had a family. You are probably earning more income than ever before; the mortgage is almost if not already paid off; and your ability to divert cash away from the household for investing has never been better.

Salary sacrificing into super

At this stage in a person's life their ability to divert earnings for wealth creation purposes should be at its greatest. Salary sacrificing $200 a week results in a reduction in spending capacity after tax, depending on a person's marginal tax rate, of between $107 a week and $137 a week, as shown in table 6.9. The benefit from this cost is total extra superannuation of between $116518 and $325185. This would mean extra tax-free income in retirement of between $134 and $375 a week.

Making large non-concessional contributions to your superannuation

When the opportunity arises it makes sense to contribute non-concessional (after-tax) funds as non-concessional contri-butions to super. This money could come from an inheritance or from selling an investment that produces a large amount of cash after tax.

Table 6.9: effect on value of superannuation of salary sacrificing $200 per week over 1 to 20 years

Marginal tax rate* (%)	Change	Weekly change ($)	Balance			
			Year 1 ($)	Year 10 ($)	Year 15 ($)	Year 20 ($)
	Increase in value of super	170.00	8840	116518	205760	325185
31.5	Reduction in after-tax spending	137.00	7124	93900	165818	262061
38.5	Reduction in after-tax spending	123.00	6396	84304	148873	235281
46.5	Reduction in after-tax spending	107.00	5564	73338	129507	204675

*This is the applicable marginal rate of tax plus Medicare levy of 1.5%.

Note: Results shown reflect an annual rate of return of 6 per cent on funds invested.

Making a non-concessional contribution to a super fund increases an individual's tax-free super benefits in that fund. If any super funds are left after the person dies, their non-dependants receive the tax-free portion without having to pay tax on it. A better after-tax benefit for someone under 60 is also achieved if they retire at 55 or if a transition to retirement pension strategy is used.

The current limit on non-concessional contributions is $150 000 a year, or $450 000 if you bring forward contributions for the next two years. Once you reach 65, non-concessional contributions are limited to $150 000 a year. It is, therefore, important to make sure the $150 000 limit is not exceeded in either of the two years before you turn 65. This will mean you can maximise your non-concessional contributions in your sixty-fifth year, if you want to.

Starting a transition to retirement pension

Since 1 July 2005, people have been able to gain access to superannuation without retiring by commencing a transition to retirement (TTR) pension. To be eligible to receive a TTR pension a person must have reached preservation age, which for most baby boomers is 55.

Other conditions relating to a TTR pension include the following:

- the pension cannot be converted into a lump sum
- the pension must be paid at a minimum rate, which varies according to the person's age
- the pension cannot be paid at a rate of more than 10 per cent of a person's superannuation balance.

The rationale behind a TTR pension is that, because super-annuation pensions receive beneficial tax treatment, a person can increase their superannuation contributions to more than offset the amount being taken as a pension.

Table 6.10 demonstrates that a person would be much better off if they salary sacrifice a contribution equal to the salary needed to produce the same after-tax result. This is because the after-tax salary sacrifice amount is greater than the TTR pension paid. The increase in superannuation is a lot more when someone is aged 60 or over and receiving a tax-free TTR pension.

Table 6.10: using a transition to retirement pension to fund contributions to super for individuals aged less than 60, and aged 60 and over

| | Marginal tax rates | | |
	30% ($)	37% ($)	45% ($)
TTR pension	20 000	20 000	20 000
Tax	6 300	7 700	9 300
Less pension offset	3 000	3 000	3 000
Tax payable on pension	3 300	4 700	6 300
Net TTR pension received after tax	16 700	15 300	13 700
Individual aged less than 60			
Pre-tax salary to produce same result	24 380	24 878	25 607
Super contribution after tax on pre-tax salary sacrificed	20 723	21 146	21 766
Gain in super per year	723	1 146	1 766
Person aged 60 or over			
Tax-free TTR pension	20 000	20 000	20 000
Pre-tax salary to produce same result	29 197	32 520	37 383
Super contribution after tax on pre-tax salary sacrificed	24 818	27 642	31 776
Gain in super per year	4 818	7 642	11 776

Combining a TTR pension strategy with non-concessional contributions to a superannuation fund produces an even better result when someone is aged less than 60, because a part of the TTR pension paid will be made up of tax-free benefits and the amount that can be salary sacrificed will be increased.

Transferring property into superannuation

Business owners who own their business premises and have a significant amount in superannuation, or have the ability to contribute large amounts, can use another strategy. For the strategy to work the business owners need to have a self managed super fund (SMSF).

SMSFs cannot purchase assets from members or their associates. One exception to this rule is business real property. Property used by a business, such as a factory or a shop, can be sold to a super fund by its members.

A condition of using this strategy is that the property must be sold at market value after a valuation has been obtained. Where the property was purchased before September 1985, no capital gains tax will be payable. For properties bought after that date, capital gains tax can be reduced by the 50 per cent general discount and the 50 per cent active assets exemption. The 50 per cent general exemption is not available if a company owns the property. In addition, the small business retirement exemption could apply to further reduce tax payable.

This strategy is a major benefit where the owners of the business have private debt. Business owners can use the proceeds of the sale of the property to substantially reduce their private debt.

Before using this strategy, professional advice should be obtained. A more complete explanation of the small business capital gains tax concessions, and the steps to take in implementing this strategy, can be found in my book *Tax for Small Business* (Wrightbooks, 2008).

Professional note

When commencing the wealth creation process, some of the main benefits are to provide alternatives and some financial basis for calculating the effect of each of those alternatives. A good example of this is a plan I did several years ago for a couple aged in their early fifties.

The husband ran a business and the wife was employed full-time. Their two sons had finished school and were both working and therefore financially independent. The couple's goals were for the wife to finish work in 12 months; the husband to sell his business in the next 18 months; and for both to retire on an income of $50 000 a year.

After taking account of all of their retirement investments and their investing capacity, I had to give them some good and bad news. The good news was that they could do what they wanted to do but the bad news was that, if they wanted $50 000 a year in retirement, their retirement investments would run out in 10 years.

I was able to offer an alternative that involved the wife ceasing full-time work now, but working part-time for another three years; the husband selling his business in 18 months, but continuing to work in the business for three years; and for them to use some of the strategies outlined in this chapter.

The result if they took this alternative was that they could retire fully in less than five years and have sufficient retirement investments to fund their desired level of income until they were well into their nineties.

Stage 5

Stage 5 is the stage immediately before or just after retirement, before you have turned 65. This is the time when the final steps can be taken to ensure you maximise your income in retirement, and invest your retirement assets to ensure they will last as long as possible.

Selling investments in a structured way

At this stage in a person's life, if they have been looking after their tax and financial affairs, it is likely that they will have investments outside of superannuation, such as property.

If the property is owned purely for investment purposes, the owner needs to consider selling the property after they have retired but before they turn 65. This is especially the case where the investment is a residential property. This is because in retirement it is important to have investments that pay a high level of income, and residential properties in most cases do not do this.

The reasons for selling the property at this time are to transfer the sale proceeds into superannuation as non-concessional (after-tax) contributions and reduce any capital gains tax impact by making a self-employed super contribution. (See chapter 3 for the rules relating to super contributions for the self-employed.) By selling and contributing to super before you turn 65, you maximise the amount you can contribute as a non-concessional contribution, as long as you have not exceeded the non-concessional $150 000 contribution limit in the previous two years.

The benefits of this strategy are that it enables you to:

- switch from taxable investment income to a tax-free superannuation pension

- sell investment assets in a structured way rather than being forced to sell them
- reduce tax payable through making a self-employed super contribution and not have to meet the work test
- increase the amount of tax-free benefits in your superannuation fund to assist with estate planning.

Before embarking on this strategy it is important to receive professional advice so that all the tax implications of selling the investment property are considered.

Making super contributions if you are self-employed

Self-employed concessional superannuation contributions can be used to reduce income tax. This strategy can be used by someone who is not receiving employer superannuation benefits because they have retired, or are living off earnings from a business or their investments.

This strategy works for people whose taxable income would be taxed at 30 per cent or more if they didn't make a self-employed super contribution. It can also apply where a person has made a large capital gain as a result of selling an investment.

Table 6.11 (overleaf) illustrates the after-tax benefit of implementing this strategy for the three higher tax levels for a $25 000 self-employed super contribution.

Taking a tax-free super payment and re-contributing

If, after you have retired and your superannuation is predominantly made up of taxable benefits, you can get some advantages by taking a lump sum superannuation payment and re-contributing it.

Table 6.11: after-tax benefit of making concessional (before-tax) superannuation contributions as a self-employed individual

	Marginal tax rate		
	30% ($)	37% ($)	45% ($)
Self-employed super contribution	25 000	25 000	25 000
Tax and Medicare levy saved by making after-tax contribution	7 875	9 625	11 625
Increase in super benefit	21 250	21 250	21 250

If you are aged less than 60, but have not taken any lump sum super payments previously, you can take $160 000 from your super fund tax-free. If you are aged 60 or more, there is no limit on the tax-free lump sum you can withdraw, but you are restricted to re-contributing only up to $450 000.

By taking a lump sum and re-contributing it into super as a non-concessional contribution you increase the tax-free percentage of your super. If you are aged less than 60 and take a pension from the super fund, a portion of that pension will be tax-free.

If you're aged 60 or more, the increase in tax-free benefits will mean that, should there be any super left when you die, this will pass to your non-dependant beneficiaries without any tax being paid on it.

Gifting and looking after the grandchildren

Gifting and looking after the grandchildren is a strategy that applies to people who have been able to organise their financial affairs so that they have more than enough investments to fund their retirement. Once an amount has been identified as being surplus to your needs, it can be used to benefit either your children or grandchildren.

Apart from just giving them the money, which may or may not provide a long-term financial benefit for them, an alternative would be to have the money contributed on their behalf to a superannuation fund as a non-concessional contribution. Your children or grandchildren might not thank you much at the time you make the gift, but when they reach retirement and they have more superannuation to fund their lifestyle they will really thank you.

For every $10000 made as a non-concessional super contribution, remembering there is a $150000 a year limit, there results an increase in superannuation, for a fund earning 6 per cent per year, of $72510 after 35 years and of almost $130000 after 45 years.

Considering a switch to an SMSF

By this stage in your financial life you should have most of your retirement assets in superannuation. If you don't have an SMSF, it may be time to consider the benefits of this type of superannuation fund (see chapter 5 for more information).

Holding your super in an SMSF will give you more control of your retirement assets, and you won't have to depend totally on the performance of other people, such as fund managers and the investment team of an industry or commercial superannuation fund. In addition, you won't face lengthy delays in accessing your accumulated retirement assets.

Before taking this step, you should seek professional advice to make sure you fully understand all the responsibilities associated with having an SMSF.

Conclusion

At this point in reading the book you should have a good understanding of your financial situation, what your investing potential is, and an understanding of the strategies you can use. It is now up to you to decide what percentage of the population you want to be in.

According to the Pareto Principle—a concept named after the Italian Vilfredo Pareto, who observed in 1906 that 80 per cent of the land in Italy was owned by 20 per cent of the population—20 per cent of the people who read this book will apply the principles described, while 80 per cent will do anything from nothing to some things to improve their ability to fund their retirement.

So the challenge for you is to start the process of controlling your finances rather than allowing your lifestyle to dictate where your money goes. This book provides you with sufficient resources to start the wealth creation process by yourself, or gives you the information to ask the right questions if you use a professional to prepare a wealth creation plan.

I will leave you with a quote from that great Vulcan wealth creation expert, Mr Spock: 'Live long and prosper'.

CHAPTER 7

Managing risk

By now you should have a good idea of your financial situation, your capacity to invest, and some ideas about the strategies that you will use. It is now important to discuss the risks you will face — if they are not properly addressed, all of your wealth creation plans could go up in smoke.

The two main risks you face are personal risk and financial risk. The impact of personal risk is relatively easy to minimise, but this does come at a cost, while managing financial risk requires a bit more work.

Personal risk and insurance

Individuals can buy many different types of insurance. Everyone knows about, and most have, risk insurance that protects their property, such as car and home insurance. The other type of risk insurance is all about protecting your most important assets: namely, you and your ability to earn an income.

Professional note

Over the many years that I've been working as a public accountant and advising people on tax and financial matters, people's attitude to insurance has always amazed me. Often they would not think twice about taking out car insurance or fire insurance for their home, but they have never considered the importance of taking out life or income protection insurance.

As most wealth creation strategies are based on people's cash flow and investing capacity, the biggest risk to the strategy not working is if the cash flow drops drastically or dries up altogether. This is why income protection insurance, especially for someone starting out on their wealth creation journey, is vital.

Income protection insurance

Payments from income protection insurance are received as an income stream to replace lost income and, because the premiums are tax-deductible, proceeds from income protection insurance are taxable.

Income protection insurance can be taken out in many ways, either directly or through a super fund. Generally, it is better to take out income protection insurance personally for the following reasons:

- the cost of income protection insurance is tax deductible and generally an individual receives a tax benefit of at least 30 per cent, whereas a superannuation fund only receives a tax deduction that results in a benefit of 15 per cent

- more extensive benefits are often available for a personally held income protection policy
- in many cases the benefit term offered by superannuation funds is only two years, while an individual can in many cases take out cover that lasts until age 65.

If income protection insurance cannot be taken out because it is unaffordable, or because a pre-existing condition means cover is not offered or is too expensive, taking it out through a superannuation fund is better than nothing.

As with most insurance products, it pays to shop around for the services of an insurance broker or financial adviser. The problem with this and other types of insurance is that advice is often given by an agent or employee who only works for one insurance company. If insurance is obtained through these traditional sources, a person may not end up with the best and most economical policy. Getting insurance advice from this source is like going to a Holden dealership and asking about the best car to buy. My guess is that you'll end up with a Holden and not an unbiased evaluation of what vehicle suits you best.

Professional note

In our practice, when we assess what insurance policies are best for a client, we have access to a system that rates insurance policies and companies. It is not unusual when using this system to find insurance policies with ratings of better than 90 per cent being significantly cheaper than policies with a lot lower rating.

Professional note *(cont'd)*

This system helps us to concentrate on the insurance companies and policies that will produce the best result for the client. Sometimes an insurance policy with fewer bells and whistles provides the client with the level of protection they need at a cost they can afford. Some insurance companies have policies aimed more at white-collar workers, where others have policies more suited to tradespeople and those involved in more manual labour.

The main factors that affect the cost of income protection insurance are:

- a person's age
- whether they are a smoker
- the monthly benefit payable
- whether the person has any pre-existing illnesses or has been injured in the past.

Generally the younger a person is, the cheaper income protection insurance will be, especially if they are in good health and do not smoke.

The level of monthly income benefit payable is dependent upon the salaries, wages or business income a person earns. In most cases insurance companies will not provide income protection insurance of more than 75 per cent of a person's income. Some companies do allow for a higher percentage of a person's income to be covered to take account of superannuation contributions.

Another factor that affects the cost of income protection insurance is the type of cover chosen. Most income protection policies offer a choice between level premiums and stepped premiums. The cost of level premiums starts out being higher than stepped premiums, but it can be considerably cheaper if the cover is maintained over the long term. This is because, while level premiums increase each year to take account of inflation, stepped premiums also increase each year to take account of the additional risk the insurer has as someone gets older.

"Rock, you I can cover. Scissors, you're too big a risk."

Source: <www.CartoonStock.com>.

The younger a person is when they take out income protection insurance the more likely it is that level cover should be chosen. This is because the older they get, the more they will need income protection insurance, when it will be at its most costly if a stepped premium is taken out.

Life insurance

If a person has borrowings, whether they are for private purposes, such as a home mortgage, or for investment reasons, the need for life insurance is almost imperative. This is especially the case for a couple, whether or not they have children.

Life insurance can, as the case with income protection insurance, be taken out as an individual or through a superannuation fund. In this instance, because life insurance is not tax deductible, it can make more sense to take out this insurance through superannuation.

To ensure that the value of your superannuation is not reduced by life insurance premiums, it can make sense to at least salary sacrifice the life insurance cost as an extra superannuation contribution.

The amount of cover required differs from person to person. At a minimum, sufficient life insurance should be taken out to at least ensure all loans and debts will be paid out upon the death of the insured. Extra cover should also be taken out if the person being insured is the main income producer, so that the insurance will pay a lump sum that can be invested and generate income to replace the income that has been lost. The amount of cover required can be reduced by the value of superannuation and investment assets.

Table 7.1 shows one way of calculating the level of life insurance required. In this example the cover is for a husband and wife, where only one person is working and there are two children. The cover is for the person who is working.

This required level of cover is a starting point. If for some reason the couple could not afford this cover, or if the spouse not currently working could get a job and earn $40 000 a year, the lump sum needed to produce the required income could be reduced. In this situation it would make sense not to deduct the value of superannuation, which would result in required cover of $312 500, and a reduction in the premium by more than half.

Another way of calculating how much life insurance is needed would be to take out insurance to cover just the loans that someone has. In this case the minimum cover required for the couple in the example would be $625 000.

Table 7.1: calculation of life insurance cover

	$	$
Debts		
Home mortgage	350 000	
Investment loan	250 000	
Car loan	25 000	
Total debts		625 000
Lump sum required to produce $40 000 in income per year at 7%		571 500
Total cover before investment assets		1 196 500
Less investment assets		
Superannuation	125 000	
Rental property	312 500	
Less total investment assets		437 500
Level of life insurance required		759 000

In the final analysis, the amount of life insurance you need depends on a multitude of factors. The cost of life insurance premiums is affected by the same sorts of things that affect income protection insurance. Just as is the case with income protection insurance, it is worth shopping around or getting professional advice on how much cover you need and what is the most cost effective for your circumstances.

Total and permanent disability insurance

Total and permanent disability (TPD) insurance is similar to life insurance in that a lump sum payment is made when the insurance event occurs. In this case, the person insured benefits from the insurance as they do not have to die for the insurance to be paid. Unfortunately they have to be classed as totally and permanently disabled and unable to work.

Professional note

One of the main factors that determine how good an insurance policy is are the definitions placed on an insurance event. An insurance event is what must happen for a payment to be made under the insurance policy.

It has often amazed me that both expensive and very cheap policies have very narrow definitions on what they regard as an insurance event. For disability and income protection insurance it is important to try to get a policy that has three definitions for when a claim will be paid.

For example, an income protection policy that only pays out when the insured cannot work at all, is not as good as a policy that pays out in the event of the insured not being able to perform the tasks and duties of their normal profession or trade.

Insurance taken out needs to cover at least the payout of any amounts owed. It can also provide a lump sum that can be used to pay for medical expenses and house alterations, and a lump sum to be invested to produce sufficient income for the individual, and possibly their family's, needs. The amount of income required may be greater in this situation as there could be the additional cost of a permanent carer.

Trauma insurance

Trauma insurance also pays a lump sum when an insurance event occurs. In this case the insurance event relates to contracting an illness or medical condition.

The object of taking out this insurance is to ensure that in the event of a person suffering a life-threatening condition (such as cancer, heart attack or stroke) sufficient funds are produced to meet medical expenses and payout liabilities. Trauma insurance can also be used to provide a lump sum to help reduce the amount of income a person needs in the event that they can no longer work.

The cost of insurance premiums for TPD and trauma insurance again differ markedly between insurance companies and policies. If you're considering this insurance you should seek professional advice.

Financial risks

Many financial risks can affect an investor. There are ways to minimise these risks. For the first and second risks discussed below, I have included the risk minimisation strategies as part of the discussion; for the others I have included the strategies at the end of this section.

Investor insanity risk

You will not find investor insanity risk in other books on investing. Sometimes this risk is called investment noise rather than being classed as a risk. I have touched on this risk in other areas and it is all about not giving in to the panic and the irrational behaviour that takes hold of investment markets and investors.

Unless you have been living on another planet until now, you will have been bombarded with information, almost on a daily basis, and more often than not with bad news, about what investment markets are doing around the world. It could be that the Dow Jones is down six points, the All

Ordinaries (All Ords) is up by two points, or pork bellies have jumped from the fat into the fire.

The fact is that the media focus too much on what is happening in investment markets. This can lead to panic and is totally irrational. This is because most people are either invested through fund managers or in direct shares, and what is happening with a market relates to all shares and not necessarily the shares you have invested in.

Getting worried about what is happening in investment markets makes as much sense, if you follow a team in the AFL or ARL, as worrying about crowd numbers attending games being down. In the end, it is how your team is doing that matters, not what is going on in the competition as a whole.

As an investor you should be concentrating on the long term. The short-term fluctuations in the market, reported in the media, although mildly interesting do not necessarily have a great effect on you. The media reporting of doom and gloom in investment markets results in panic selling, which smart investors see as an opportunity for buying, not selling. Over-optimistic predictions that lead to a market boom result in shares becoming overvalued, which should be seen as an opportunity to sell.

Currency risk

Currency risk affects overseas investments (such as property, shares and loans) where their value and return can increase or decrease depending on how the value of the Australian dollar moves in relation to the overseas currency used for the investment.

With the depressed state of the US dollar and the US real estate market in recent times, some people have been looking at the possibility of investing in the US property market. The impact of currency risk can be best explained by the example of someone who purchased a property in the US before the GFC.

If a property cost US$300 000 and was purchased when the Australian dollar purchased only 80 US cents, it would have taken A$375 000 to pay for the investment. If the property was later sold for US$350 000, when one Australian dollar equalled one US dollar, the investor would suffer a loss of A$25 000.

This situation can also apply where other investments, such as shares, are purchased in a foreign currency. Because the movement in currency exchange rates is outside the control of most individual investors, apart from maintaining a bank account in the currency of the investment, there's not much an investor can do to avoid this risk.

Large institutions and fund managers have the ability to buy insurance against fluctuations in currency, using strategies such as hedging, but like all insurance this comes at a cost. Sometimes the cost of hedging an overseas investment against currency risk can be greater than the actual currency exchange rate cost.

Inflation risk

Inflation in the past was a major problem. During the 1970s and 1980s Australia experienced inflation rates that were so high that they were solved only by the recession we had to have. From a high for inflation of 15.3 per cent in 1974, the rate fluctuated wildly, but tended to be mainly in the range of 7 to 9 per cent.

The impact of inflation on those in employment is nowhere near as great as the impact on those who are retired and/or living off income from investments. This is because the salaries and wages of the employed tend to increase at a greater rate than inflation, while investment income can actually drop or increase at a lesser rate than inflation.

The impact of inflation, and the fact that average weekly earnings have more than kept pace with inflation, was illustrated in an article prepared by the Australian Bureau of Statistics in 2001. The article covered the period from 1901 to 2000 and showed the effect of inflation, and how much the average weekly wage for an adult male had increased, over those 100 years. Table 7.2 shows that the average weekly wage for an adult male if it had increased in line with inflation would have been $217.50 in 2000, but actually stood at $830. In some cases, the increase in costs, such for as bread, was also much greater than the inflation rate, while the cost of some basic food items had not increased anywhere near as much as they would have as a result of inflation.

Since 2000 Australia's inflation rate has not been higher than 4.48 per cent, but this does not mean inflation is not a problem for someone who is trying to fund their retirement. The real impact of inflation affects investors who have too much of their funds in defensive, income-producing investments.

Although defensive assets usually produce greater income returns than growth assets, their value does not increase over time in the way that the value of growth assets, such as shares, do. This means as prices increase because of inflation the amount of income being produced stays the same because the capital value of the defensive investment has not increased.

Table 7.2: comparison of the increase in average weekly earnings for males with the increase in inflation and actual costs for basic food and housing, 1901–2000

	1901 actual prices ($)	1901 prices after 100 years of inflation ($)	2000 actual prices ($)
Average weekly wage, adult males	4.35	217.50	830.00
Loaf of bread	0.02	1.00	2.30
Coffee (150 g)	0.05	2.50	6.00
Tea (180 g)	0.06	3.00	3.40
Butter (500 g)	0.13	6.50	2.00
Potatoes (1 kg)	0.02	1.00	1.30
Rump steak (1 kg)	0.14	7.00	12.50
Eggs (1 dozen)	0.12	6.00	2.90
Milk (1 litre)	0.03	1.50	1.40
Rent on three-bedroom house (1 week)	1.30	65.00	250.00
Concert	0.75	37.50	39.30
Game of football	0.10	5.00	21.70

Source: Australian Bureau of Statistics, 'Prices in Australia at the beginning and end of the 20th century', *Year Book Australia, 2001.*

Interest rate risk

There has never been a better example of the impact of interest rate risk than the effect of falling interest rates on retirees as a result of the GFC. Many investors who had been earning between 6 and 8 per cent as a fixed interest return saw their income slashed when interest rates dropped to less than 3 per cent.

A rising or falling interest rate market not only causes income levels to fluctuate, fluctuations can also affect the value of some fixed interest investments. If someone is forced to sell a fixed interest investment that is paying a low interest rate when rates are rising, the value of the investment will have fallen (because few people will want to buy a fixed interest investment that offers a low interest rate), and a loss can be made.

Liquidity risk

Liquidity risk is running out of cash. If liquidity risk is not handled properly, it can be the greatest cause of investment loss. While accumulating assets for retirement, insufficient cash can result in an investment having to be sold to pay interest, pay other costs or, if a finance company requires it, repay a debt. Where a person has insufficient cash to fund their living expenses in retirement, or not have enough cash in their super pension account to fund minimum pension payments, investments must be sold to produce the cash required. A person can then be forced to sell an investment at a loss to produce the cash. The first choice would be to sell investments that are liquid, in other words, that can be easily converted to cash. An example is shares, which can be sold on the share market and the investor needs to sell only enough shares to meet the shortfall.

Australia's love affair with property as an investment class can have serious consequences in this situation, because property is not a liquid investment—it can't readily be converted to cash. If, for example, income stops because a tenant leaves, the income required for the retiree's living expenses will also stop. It is impossible to produce extra income by selling the odd brick or weatherboard to make up the shortfall—the whole asset must be sold, and the owner may have to accept a lower price for a quick sale.

Market risk

Market risk is what is associated with assets that are purchased and sold via a market. The risk comes because these markets are by their nature unstable and values increase and decrease.

This is the risk that, until the GFC, most Australians will have not fully understood—except those old enough to have lived through the Great Depression. Investment markets are not perfect and in many cases are driven more by emotion and sentiment than by logic and facts. For this reason, the value of investments traded on a market can fluctuate wildly. When there are large falls in the value of investments at a time when a retiree needs cash, investment losses are inevitable.

Market timing risk

Market timing risk only applies to people who don't have an investment crystal ball. Nonetheless, many people think they can predict when markets are going to go up and when they are going to fall. This can lead to investments being sold too early when values keep rising. It can also lead to large losses when investments are held for too long in a falling market and markets crash.

Diversification risk

Diversification risk can work in two ways. The return and value of an investment portfolio that is not diversified enough, and therefore concentrated in one class of investment or just one investment in each class, can be adversely affected by fluctuations in the value of that class or investment.

Where someone over-diversifies their investments within each asset class, the cost of administering the investments can outweigh the benefits of diversification. In addition, where investments are diversified across many fund managers, it would have been better to invest in an index fund because, by over-diversifying, that is effectively what someone ends up with.

Reducing risk

Risks associated with investing can be reduced in three ways.

The first relates to the length of time an investment is held. The longer an investment is owned, the lower the risk that it will fall in value. Despite the wild gyrations of the Australian sharemarket over recent and distant history, a loss has never been produced over a 10-year rolling average period. This means that if you take the results for the Australian sharemarket over any consecutive 10-year period the average return produced for each 10 years produced a positive return.

The time an investment is held especially helps reduce the risk of market timing. Where a conscious decision is made to buy an investment and hold it for the long term, no matter what the markets are doing, the chances of making a loss are reduced. An old investment saying is, 'It is the time in markets that makes the money, not trying to time the markets'.

The second means of reducing risk is diversification. Diversification means investing in all six different investment classes—cash, fixed interest, property, Australian shares, international shares and alternatives — and also diversifying within each investment class.

The third means of reducing risk relates to regularly rebalancing your investment portfolio. A person's age and tolerance of investment risk determine what percentage they should have in each of the six investment classes. Once the percentage limits for each investment have been set, investors need to stick to this plan. For a more detailed explanation of the percentage holdings for each different asset class see chapter 8.

The biggest risks of all

Up until this point I have mainly been looking at how risk affects investments and how to reduce the impact of these risks. Two of the biggest risks we all face are that of not being able to look after our own affairs because we have become incapacitated or died. These risks not only affect our financial life, they can also have a major impact on our personal life and on the lives of those who depend on us. Thankfully some legal steps can be taken to reduce the impact of both of these events.

Incapacity

If a person becomes incapable of looking after their own affairs, possibly due to illness, an accident or a medical condition, such as dementia or stroke, there are two possible alternatives. Those who have not anticipated this risk can find control of their financial affairs is taken over by a trustee company at great financial cost, or their loved ones are forced into a nightmare of bureaucracy to be allowed to look after their financial affairs.

The second alternative is not costly or complicated, and that is to have an enduring power of attorney drawn up, appointing your partner or someone else you trust to look after your affairs. In addition, consideration should be given to having a medical power of attorney drawn up so that if you don't want your life prolonged artificially in the event of your being brain dead, someone is authorised to make that decision on your behalf.

Simple powers of attorney can be obtained from many sources, such as legal stationers and the internet, but if you have a number of investment structures or investments, serious consideration should be given to having a power of attorney drawn up by a suitably experienced lawyer.

Professional note

Many years ago the impact of someone not putting in place an enduring power of attorney was brought home when I had an appointment with a new client. It was with a lady in her late fifties who was wearing a scarf to hide the evidence of hair loss from chemotherapy.

She told me that her husband had recently suffered a major stroke that meant he could no longer look after his own affairs. Despite dealing with her own health problems she was now required to make an application before a board that would allow her to administer the financial affairs of her husband.

In addition to completing a lengthy document detailing all of her husband's finances she had to appear before the board to be appointed his trustee. She also had to complete an annual report every year, with our involvement and assistance, which was lodged with the board to show that she was not ripping off her husband. All of this cost and work could have been avoided if her husband had given her an enduring power of attorney.

Death

I am often amazed by how many of my clients have not prepared a will. Perhaps this is because going through the process of preparing a will can be too much of a reminder of their mortality. Given the complications and unnecessary expense that occurs when a person dies intestate (without a will), this is a job that should not be put off until it's too late.

The need for a will is even more important when a person has a large amount of financial assets—through having implemented wealth creation strategies, superannuation or life insurance—or has a young family. In either situation serious consideration should be given to having a will drawn up by a lawyer specialising in this area.

In chapter 4 I stressed the importance of reducing the marginal rate of tax payable as much as possible on income earned. The importance of this can be even more critical after the death of a parent to ensure the financial security of the surviving parent and child(ren).

If a very simple will is drawn up and all the financial assets of the deceased are left to the surviving spouse, all the income earned from those assets will be taxed in the hands of that spouse at their relevant marginal tax rate.

An alternative to this is to have a more complicated will prepared that sets up a testamentary trust for the benefit of the children. In this situation the income earned from the assets passing to the testamentary trust are taxed in the hands of the children as if they were adults. An example of this strategy would be the death of a 45-year-old husband who has investments, life insurance and superannuation totalling $700 000. If all of this was left to his wife and it produced an income of $50 000 she would pay tax of $8550 per year.

If a testamentary trust had been set up for his two children, with $200 000 of investments passing to it, and it earned $15 000 in income, no tax would be paid on this income by the children, and his wife would only pay $4350 in tax on the $35 000 of income she earned on the remainder of the capital ($500 000). This would result in an increase of more than $4000 in disposable income for the family. There would be a further decrease in tax payable due to the increased low income tax offset the wife would receive.

Assets left to children in a testamentary trust must become theirs eventually, depending on the conditions attached to the testamentary trust.

There are some other things that must be taken into account when preparing a will, which is why it is important to get advice from a lawyer who specialises in this area.

Death and super

Another aspect of preparing for the inevitability of death relates to superannuation. First, investments held in a superannuation fund do not form part of a person's estate and in some cases a deceased's wishes can be ignored. Where superannuation will end up depends on where the trustees of the super fund decide to pay the benefits or, where a binding death benefit nomination exists, this will decide where or to whom the superannuation is paid.

An example of this was a recent court case surrounding a substantial sum of money held by a deceased in a self managed super fund. At the time of death, the other fund member and trustee of the SMSF was the deceased's son. After his father's death his son had his wife join the super fund as a member and trustee. He then assumed full ownership of all the assets in the superannuation fund without compensating his sister, who had not been a member of the SMSF.

Despite the father's will requiring that his estate be split equally between his two children, the court ruled that as superannuation did not form part of the estate the brother was able to keep all of his misbegotten gains.

If you are concerned that something like this could happen to you, a simple way to overcome this is to complete a binding death benefit nomination. This will force the trustees of a superannuation fund to act in accordance with your wishes.

When a person dies with taxable benefits in super, and they are paid to non-dependant beneficiaries, tax is paid by the beneficiaries at the rate of 15 per cent on taxed benefits and 30 per cent on untaxed benefits. If, however, a person aged 60 or more withdraws most of their super before their death and gives the funds to their children, no tax is paid by the fund, them as a fund member, or their children.

There are personal and income tax problems if this action is taken without proper advice. In the first instance, if it is not done correctly the super fund could end up paying capital gains tax unnecessarily. In the second instance, if the timing is wrong and the amount given away is too much, the super fund member will have to survive on the generosity of their children who now own most of their parent's financial assets.

The main point to remember is when it comes to death there is nothing to be gained by ignoring it. If, however, the proper steps are taken the financial impact of death on the people you love and care about is minimised.

CHAPTER 8

Understanding investments

The final step in the process of funding your retirement is selecting your investments, whether you invest directly or through a superannuation fund. If investments are made outside superannuation, investment can be direct (such as buying shares or property) or indirect (made through a listed or unlisted managed fund).

When you invest through a superannuation fund, other than a self managed super fund (SMSF), your investment choice will depend on what is offered by the trustee of that fund. Whatever your situation, it is important to have a basic understanding of the different asset classes and the investments in each class.

I am not going to tell you how to become a self-made millionaire by following some investment selection or accumulation process known only to me. If I had one dollar for every investor who has paid money to some so-called property, share or futures trading guru to learn how to get rich quick, I would be able to retire tomorrow a very rich person. The sad truth about many of these so-called investing systems is that the promoters of the systems usually make a lot more money than the investors do — not by investing cleverly, but from sucking in the unwary to pay them for the 'secrets of investing'.

Professional note

Over the years of practising as a public accountant I have met many people who have signed up for various types of investing systems. My stated aim for clients has always been to maximise their income while minimising the tax they pay. Of the clients who paid good money to be shown how to become rich, not one of them needed help with paying tax on huge profits — in most cases they broke even at best.

I hope by this stage of the book you recognise that, apart from striking it lucky with lotto or the lotteries, there is no such thing as a single investment that produces a 100 per cent financial solution. Instead, it's all about taking a disciplined approach to your finances and looking for, and implementing, the 100 one per cent wealth creation solutions.

Lessons from history

This chapter is about equipping you with some basic information about how markets and investments work. To do this it is important to take a lesson from history. When you look back at recent and not so recent investing history you will understand that the cycles of boom and bust have been with us for a very long time, and the mistakes made in the past are often repeated later on.

In the late 1800s the Australian economy was based on the natural resource of wool, and British banks and foreign investment capital supplied the money that supported the industry. At the same time, the banking crisis in the United Kingdom during the 1890s led to an extreme tightening of credit; the Australian economy declined because of falling wool prices; and many borrowers defaulted on loans.

The effect of the collapse on the fledgling Australian banking industry was catastrophic. Many banks failed and others suspended paying out depositors for more than 10 years. The big difference between that collapse and the turmoil of the global financial crisis (GFC) is that the government of the day did not step in and guarantee bank deposits—though the economic wisdom of this step taken by the Rudd Labor government is still in doubt with many advisers and people in the funds management industry believing it caused panic selling of non-guaranteed investments.

The Australian banking collapse of the late 1800s and the GFC both demonstrate that investment markets, by their nature, are unsettled. There will always be times of relative stability, but there will also be times when markets get over-heated and overvalued, and times when panic sets in, markets crash and investments become undervalued.

Most of the data on market crashes relates to the United States and a look back reinforces the fact that booms and busts are a natural part of investing. Since 1825 the US stock market has experienced 26 crashes of more than 10 per cent of value, and 84 years of growth exceeding 10 per cent. These facts not only reinforce existence of the boom and bust cycles in sharemarkets, but also reassure me that, even with the recent experience of the GFC, growth years outnumber crashes almost four to one.

Listed overleaf are the 10 worst stock market crashes on the New York Stock Exchange. The fact that there are 10 of them is not surprising as this is what happens after a sharemarket goes through a boom period.

What is surprising is that investors over the last 130 years seem to be ignorant of the boom and bust cycle that is a natural part of sharemarkets. It is also interesting that often the cause of the crash is not unique but is repeated time and time again. The lesson for investors is to not be caught up in the hype of a boom and not get panicked by the gloom of a crash.

The 10 worst stock market crashes on the New York Stock Exchange since 1900

Following are the 10 worst stock market crashes on the New York Stock Exchange since 1900 and their causes:

- *10th worst crash: 2000–2002.* Key events: tech bubble burst; 11 September 2000 terrorist attacks in the US. Total loss: –37.8 per cent.

- *9th worst crash: 1916–1917.* Key events: US was drawn into the First World War. Total loss: –40.1 per cent.

- *8th worst crash: 1939–1942.* Key events: Second World War; Japanese attack on Pearl Harbor. Total loss: –40.4 per cent.

- *7th worst crash: 1973–1974.* Key events: Vietnam War; Watergate scandal. Total loss: –45.1 per cent.

- *6th worst crash: 1901–1903.* Key events: assassination of US president William McKinley; a severe drought causing alarm about US food supplies. Total loss: –46.1 per cent.

- *5th worst crash: 1919–1921.* Key events: postwar boom is followed by a crash; bursting of the big automobile sector tech bubble where the market had been driven up by exuberance for the technological wonder of the time. Total loss: –46.6 per cent.

- *4th worst crash: 1929.* Key events: the New York Stock Exchange had increased almost 400 per cent from

1926 to 1929, banks relaxed credit terms that led to investors borrowing heavily to join the stock market boom, negative consumer sentiment led to a contracting economy, there was a decline in real estate values, then panic set in resulting in more than three times the normal number of shares being sold on the one day, Black Thursday, which was the start of the crash and brought an end to the roaring twenties and kicked off the Great Depression. Total loss: –47.9 per cent.

- *3rd worst crash: 1906–1907.* Key events: the Bankers Panic of 1907, which came at a time of economic recession, several state and local banks failed, other banks tightened lending practises that led to a shortage of cash, resulting in panic selling. Total loss: –48.5 per cent.

- *2nd worst crash: 1937–1938.* Key events: after almost a 50 per cent recovery in losses from the Great Depression, fear of war breaking out in Europe and several Wall Street scandals relating to the misappropriation of funds. Total loss: –49.1 per cent

- *Worst crash: 1930–1932.* Investors lost 86 per cent of their money over 813 days. Combined with the 1929 crash, this period makes up the Great Depression. Total loss: –86.0 per cent.

This list was prepared before the GFC. During the GFC, over a period of 18 months the Dow Jones industrial average went from a high of 14 280 on 8 October 2007, to a low of 6626 on 9 March 2009, a fall of 53.6 per cent, making this the second worst US stock market crash.

At the time of writing, the Dow Jones industrial average was standing at 11 872, an increase from the low of just over

79 per cent. This reinforces an important lesson to learn from investing: when markets get overvalued, that is the time to consider selling, when everyone else is buying. When markets are being oversold, and they are at historical lows, that is the time to consider buying, when everyone else is selling.

Boom and bust cycles

A very good book on investing is *The Four Pillars of Investing* by William J Bernstein. In the book, Bernstein puts forward what he thinks it takes to deliver long-term investment returns. As a part of this he uses history to explain the reason why markets react the way they do. In the chapter detailing past boom and bust sharemarkets, going back as far as the 1687 English sharemarket that revolved around speculation on companies involved in finding Spanish treasure that led to a crash, Bernstein puts forward four common conditions for sharemarket booms and crashes. They are:

- a major technological revolution or shift in financial practice
- easy credit
- amnesia about the last bubble
- abandonment of time-honoured methods of security valuation.

What this study of past booms and crashes shows is that history does repeat itself and that after every crash there is a recovery. The recent experience of the GFC is no exception. The recovery may not be immediate, and inevitably there are long periods of instability, but in the end the markets return to a period of being settled that will inevitably be followed by the next boom and bust cycle.

Investing history also shows that each of the different asset classes — shares, property and bonds — goes through its own cycle of booms and busts. Investors need to learn a lesson eloquently spelt out in Bernstein's book, which is that having a balance of investments across the different asset classes is what produces long-term wealth.

Bernstein distrusts markets to the point where he advocates investing in index funds rather than trying to pick companies and fund managers that you hope will outperform the sharemarket as a whole. This is where Bernstein and I have a difference of opinion. I tend to follow the principles of investing espoused by famous investor Warren Buffett. He believes that markets over-react and there are times when good investments can be purchased at relatively cheap prices. I do, however, believe that a combination of direct investments mixed with an index fund can provide opportunities during the boom and bust cycles.

The importance of balance

Whenever you talk about health, one of the most important contributing factors is said to be balance. Relationships and mental health depend on striking a balance between work, play and family. Life expectancy and our personal health depend on our having a balanced diet and a balance between being a couch potato and a marathon runner.

Financial health depends on getting the balance right between income received and money spent and, depending on your age and stage of life, a balance between the different asset classes. This balance between the different asset classes is vitally important when a person depends on their retirement assets to produce an income.

Personal note

I have been around now for almost 60 years and have been investing for more than 45 years. Most of this chapter is drawn from my own investing experiences. Over that time I've enjoyed many investment successes, while at times I've been caught up in booms and, like everyone else, had some investment losses.

My initial exposure to the Australian sharemarket came as a result of the generosity of my maternal grandfather. This took the form of a gift of 1000 shares in a company called Rocla. In the mid 1960s a takeover bid was made for Rocla, resulting in the share price doubling. At about the same time my brother and I had been thinking about buying a billiard table. We each sold half of our Rocla shares and bought a billiard table from the proceeds. Not long after this Rocla had a two-for-one issue of shares to fight the takeover bid, and we ended up with the same number of shares as before. It is not hard to see why at that point I thought that investing in shares was a great wealth accumulation strategy.

This success was followed by others, but there have also been failures along the way. Like being caught up in the dotcom boom and buying a share that was all promise and no substance, and investing in a fancy derivative investment fund that collapsed.

These two experiences reinforced for me the importance of diversification across the different investment asset classes and within each investment asset class. As a result of limiting the amount of money I had in these two investments, although I lost money, these losses were offset by gains in other investments.

The last thing any investor wants to be forced to do is sell an investment. This can happen when funds have been borrowed to finance an investment and the lender demands some of the principal be repaid. It can also happen when the income generated by investments is insufficient to support the lifestyle you want, and some must be sold to generate the cash required.

You do not need to look for proof of this problem back further than just before 2008. Many self-funded retirees had been led to believe the sharemarket boom would go on forever, and a high percentage of their investment portfolios were in shares. The Rudd Labor government, recognising that further sharemarket chaos would result if retirees were forced to sell their shares to generate cash to fund pensions, halved the minimum age pension rates.

You must, therefore, understand that when you have too much of your available funds invested in one asset class, such as shares, the damage can be catastrophic when things go wrong.

The need to have a balanced view of investing has been supported by many sources over the years. There is a point of view that states, 'More value is added to a person's wealth by getting the balance right between the different asset classes than is added by investment selection'. In other words deciding on the percentage you will allocate to each asset class, and regularly rebalancing your portfolio, will add more value overall than trying to pick what is going to be the next best share to invest in or who is the best fund manager for your cash.

Table 8.1 (overleaf) demonstrates that the returns for the different asset classes from 1990 to 2009 vary to such an extent that they can be the best performing investment in some years while in others be the worst performing — even from one year to the next.

Table 8.1: best and worst performers among major asset classes, 1990–2009

Year	Best performing class	Worst performing class
1990	Fixed interest	Australian shares
1991	Australian shares	Cash
1992	Fixed interest	Australian shares
1993	Australian shares	Cash
1994	Cash	Australian shares
1995	International shares	Cash
1996	Listed property	International shares
1997	International shares	Cash
1998	International shares	Cash
1999	Australian shares	Listed property
2000	Listed property	International shares
2001	Listed property	International shares
2002	Listed property	International shares
2003	Australian shares	International shares
2004	Listed property	Cash
2005	Australian shares	Cash
2006	Listed property	Fixed interest
2007	Australian shares	Listed property
2008	Fixed interest	Listed property
2009	Australian shares	Global shares

Source: © Financial Security Services Pty Ltd, February 2011.
Asset Classes: Can I expect last year's best investment to be this year's winner?
<http://www.financialsecurity.com.au/images/stories/educational/asset_classes_feb_2011.pdf>.

The asset classes

In my investment universe I split investment assets into four classes or categories:

- defensive or income assets
- growth assets
- defensive growth assets
- alternative assets.

Each asset class has its own income and risk characteristics —the secret is to blend them depending on your tolerance to risk or what financial stage you are in life.

A principle that applies to many things definitely applies to these different asset classes: 'The greater the risk that something has, the greater the potential return'. That's the same as working for an employer in a secure position without the potential for the above-average income that you might earn if you took the risk of owning and operating your own business.

In the investment world, cash and fixed interest are regarded as being a lot less risky than shares and property. In normal circumstances the increased risk associated with buying shares and property results in a superior return, including both income and capital growth.

Once the current turmoil in investment markets is over and the world's economies have recovered, it will be hoped that the status quo returns, with the returns from shares and property once again being higher than returns from the more conservative investments.

In most cases my interpretation of these different asset classes is similar to traditional approaches. It is an unfortunate fact that when most people seek advice on investments the advice they receive is biased. If they are speaking to a stockbroker, the advice will be heavily weighted towards direct shares, while a real estate agent's advice is biased toward property. When many people seek advice from financial planners, the advice is biased towards managed funds and wrap accounts in general, and often more specifically only those managed funds and wrap accounts that the adviser is associated with.

In the following explanation of the different types of investments I try to drill down to the underlying investments and how they behave.

Defensive assets

Defensive investments, also known as income assets, are meant mainly to produce income without much, if any, fluctuation in their value. These assets include fixed interest investments, such as government and corporate bonds, term deposits, mortgages, first mortgages and cash. The reason they are called defensive is because most investors believe that the value of the investment is secure. The truth is that some fixed interest investments can decrease in value, just like growth investments.

An example of this is government or corporate bonds. In many cases these investments are for a fixed term at a fixed rate of interest. When interest rates start rising the underlying value of the investment can decrease because people don't want to pay full price for this investment when they can get better deals elsewhere. If an investor is forced to sell one of these investments before it matures, they can suffer a loss. Conversely, when interest rates are falling, the underlying value of an investment with a fixed high rate of return will be greater than new investments at a lower interest rate, and they can be sold at a profit.

In addition to the value of one of these investments decreasing because of rising interest rates, investors can suffer a loss when the borrower (issuer of the investment) defaults and the underlying value of the asset is less than the loan value.

Investing into this asset class can be direct, such as taking out a term deposit or investing directly in a first mortgage, or indirectly, such as through a unitised investment in listed and unlisted trusts. In addition, investment can be made through index funds, which buy up the investments making up an index. Examples of these in the fixed interest area are the UBS Australian Composite Bond Index and the Barclays Capital Global Aggregate ex Securitised Index.

Growth assets

Growth assets are expected to produce some income, but most of the return should come from an increase in their value. The value of these investments is often dictated by the principles of supply and demand, which can come from their being listed on an exchange, such as shares, or from an open market, as is the case with property. A feature of this investment class is that the underlying value of an investment is not always reflected in its market value.

Because the sharemarket goes through boom and bust cycles, in a lot of cases other investments in this class do so too. The secret when investing in growth assets is not allowing yourself to get caught up in the hype of whatever is driving a particular market. Instead, keep a clear head and make decisions based on your long-term wealth creation goals.

As Warren Buffett puts it, 'Look at market fluctuations as your friend rather than your enemy; profit from folly rather than participate in it'. Another principle of Buffett's is to buy when everyone else is selling, and sell when everyone else is buying. Putting it another way, when a market crashes it is best not to jump off the cliff with the other lemmings and sell in a panic—it is a lot better to be the hawk spotting and buying undervalued investments.

Growth assets are predominantly shares in companies listed on the Australian and overseas sharemarkets. You can invest in Australian shares in four ways:

- through direct share investment
- through a managed fund
- through an index fund
- through a separately managed account (SMA).

Direct share investment

Investing directly in the sharemarket can be very rewarding when the shares are held for the long term. During the boom that preceded the GFC, many investors became day traders, buying and selling shares regularly for short-term profit. When a market is rising, it is not too difficult to make a profit doing this. Unfortunately, as many investors learnt, when a market crashes this approach can lead to major losses.

When I buy shares in a listed company I tend to look for the business that is paying dividends from earnings and represents good value. To help me identify these investment opportunities, I download the industrial share list in spreadsheet form. I then sort all the companies shown based on the earnings per share (EPS). Any companies that show a negative amount — indicating they made a loss — is deleted. I next sort the companies on the basis of their net tangible asset backing (NTA), or the total value of the company's assets, less liabilities divided by the number of issued shares. Companies that have a negative NTA are deleted, as their liabilities exceed their assets. The next sort I do is based on the dividend yield of the company. Depending on market conditions, I then delete shares with a dividend yield of less than 4 per cent.

For all the companies that remain I then delete any that are either distributing as dividends more than the earnings per share, which means they are using asset sales or borrowings to fund the dividends, or distributing nearly all of their earnings as dividends. A well-managed company should retain a reasonable proportion of their earnings to help grow the business or reduce debt to help protect it in times of economic downturn.

I then look at such things as the share price compared with the NTA, and where the current share price was within the last 52 weeks trading range. The object is to identify well-run, profitable companies that are selling at a discount. This is only the start of the process. From here the work of researching exactly what the company does, the strength and experience of the management, and what their market advantage or disadvantage is, needs to be completed before I decide whether a share is worth buying.

Personal note

No methodology that identifies individual listed companies to buy is foolproof. Using my methodology in September 2008 identified a number of investment opportunities. These included the banks, which have since continued paying high dividends and increased in value, but also included some companies that had major problems.

As I am investing for the long term, companies that have not performed as I had anticipated have been kept hoping for an eventual turnaround when the economy improves. In other cases, where I have felt strongly enough about the company, I have since purchased more shares at a much reduced price, thus averaging my cost.

Whatever system you use to decide which shares to invest directly in — whether that be following your share broker's recommendations, subscribing to one of the more reputable share reporting services, or from doing your own research — the important thing to remember is to diversify your investment over a number of listed companies that you plan to hold for the long term.

If you also want to be involved in some short-term share speculation, or want to follow the latest share tips from your mates at a barbecue or from a taxi driver, limit your exposure to this area to no more than 10 per cent of all of your total net worth or the amount you have allocated to invest in shares.

Managed funds: active and index

An alternative to investing directly in the sharemarket is to use a managed fund. Where a person does not have a lot to invest, or they are using a regular dollar cost averaging investment strategy, managed share funds can be a benefit.

Managed share funds are split into two types: passive (or index) and active. A share index is a method of measuring the performance of the whole of a sharemarket, such as the Australian All Ordinaries Index or a sector of the market, such as the top 200 companies by size. An index fund invests in the shares that make up the index, so you will have automatic diversification across many shares for a small amount of money.

Index funds tend to be very large, as they hold all or nearly all the companies that make up the index. The fund manager doesn't have to do any research to work out what companies to buy, so the management fee charged by these fund managers tends to be very low.

Active fund managers hold a much smaller number of companies and they are meant to thoroughly research companies before buying or selling them. This extra work (and the extra staff to do the work) means the fee charged by active managers is higher than an index fund manager's fees. This increased fee is meant to be offset by their funds earning more than an index fund does.

The unfortunate truth is that many fund managers say they are active, charge active manager fees, but make too many of their buy and sell decisions based on movements in an index. Active fund managers are supposed to buy companies that are undervalued and sell companies either because they are overvalued or because it is time to take a profit.

Within the Australian sharemarket, investors can incre-ase diversification by not just investing in the top 200 comp-anies. Some managed funds invest in mid-sized companies and also in the small company sector. The small company sector carries a larger risk, but at times it has produced higher returns.

If you think that investing in Australian shares is complicated because of the choices, the overseas share sector has an almost endless amount of choices. It is rare for Australian investors to buy directly into companies listed on overseas sharemarkets. The more common way to invest in this asset class is through managed funds.

This is where the range of choice can be confusing and, for the unwary, can lead to losses. Some international share funds have very little exposure to anything but the American sharemarket, while other funds can have highly concentrated share holdings in other geographic areas, such as Asia or Europe.

The differences between active and index Australian managed funds also applies to international share funds. There are also some that pretend to be active, but are in fact benchmark huggers that add very little value. These managers are more concerned about protecting their business risk than actively managing a share portfolio on behalf of their investors.

Separately managed accounts

An alternative to managed funds is separately managed accounts (SMAs). When an investment is made through a managed fund, the manager decides what companies to buy and sell, and it owns the shares it has purchased. In an SMA the investor still gives an amount of money to a fund manager to invest on their behalf, but the shares are purchased in the name of the investor.

The benefits of SMAs are:

- the shares are owned by the investor

- if the fund manager is changed the taxable capital gains impact is reduced, compared with selling a managed fund
- the investor knows what shares are being bought and sold by the manager
- if the fund manager's decisions are not made on sound investment principles, but appear more to be made as a result of movements in an index, the investor can look for a more active manager.

Defensive growth assets

You won't find defensive growth assets as an asset class in many books on investing. I have come up with this term for only one asset because it has the income characteristics of a defensive asset, but also exhibits the characteristics of a growth asset. This asset is also the investment of choice for many Australians. It is direct property.

The financial management and planning industries have for many years classed property as a growth asset. Given Australians' love affair with property investments, and the belief that bricks and mortar are one of the safest investments a person can have, lumping property in with the other growth assets is doing it a disservice.

One of the reasons for property being classed as a growth asset is because the finance industry classes listed property trusts as a property investment, and in most cases does not take into account investments in direct property or unlisted property trusts.

Listed property trusts

Listed property trusts (LPTs) originally started as property-based investments, with their income being generated from rent, and their capital growth from the increase in value of the properties held. But over many years that changed. LPTs should now be regarded as a subset of the All Ordinaries Index, like the mining and retail sectors, rather than being classed as a property investment.

In too many cases LPTs have invested less and less in direct property, and have often become property developers. In addition to owning property and developing property, they also often invest in other listed property trusts. Over time a smaller percentage of their income has come from rent, and an increasing percentage has come from dividends, distributions from other property trusts, and property development profits. They also often borrow heavily to finance their acquisitions or developments, opening themselves up to the risks associated with having too much debt.

Traditionally the value of an LPT was determined by the value of the property or properties owned by the trust. Now, however, the value of LPTs is decided by the number of buyers and sellers in the sharemarket. For proof of this fact you need look no further back than five years. Leading up to the GFC, listed property trusts, because of their superior income yields, became very popular and their prices soared on the stock market. In many cases, the price being paid per unit far exceeded the net tangible asset value of each unit. In many cases the superior return did not come from net rental income or profits: it came from borrowed funds. As soon as the credit crisis started, many LPTs were put under severe financial pressure by their lenders. In the GFC crash, the value of LPTs was slashed by more than 60 per cent between 2006 and 2008. Some of the better managed trusts were trading at a price well below their net tangible asset backing.

Unlisted property trusts

If you do not have sufficient funds or borrowing capacity to invest directly into property, you can invest in this asset class through unlisted property trusts. These trusts have the characteristics of a defensive investment because they produce regular income but, unlike other defensive assets that are not expected to produce a capital gain, they can increase in value and produce capital gains, just like growth assets. Unfortunately, like other growth assets, they can also produce losses.

Another characteristic of unlisted property trusts that makes them very much a growth asset is that they should be held for at least five years and they are illiquid. Liquidity, or the lack of it, is another reason for making sure that you get the balance right when putting together your investment portfolio for retirement. Because a property investment is illiquid, or can't be readily converted to cash, it does not make sense to allocate more than 30 per cent of your available funds when retired to this asset class. In addition, rather than investing in one direct property, it makes sense to invest in several unlisted property trusts to reduce the risk.

Losses from a property investment tend to come when a person has got the balance of their investments wrong and they are forced to sell.

Alternative assets

Alternative assets are often included as part of an investment portfolio to provide some protection from sharp movements in traditional investment markets. Their performance should not be affected by the performance of other investment classes. Often they aren't traded on an organised exchange, or are otherwise difficult to access for the average investor.

Alternative assets include commodities, natural resources, private equity, venture capital and agribusiness investments. They also include hedge funds, which employ different strategies that aim to make profits from the sharemarket, whether it is going up or going down. Originally, few managers operated in the hedge fund and alternatives area, which meant funds were producing above-average returns. Unfortunately, this superior investment performance led to many fund management companies jumping into the sector, which then became overcrowded, and as a result, investment returns for hedge funds were severely reduced.

The alternative asset class can carry with it a higher level of risk than other investments, but the reason to include them in a portfolio is to provide an investment return that is not dependent on the factors that affect other investment classes. You do need to be careful when investing in this sector, as some fund managers and promoters of alternative investments, such as hedge funds, make it almost impossible for the investor to work out what they are doing.

"In the beginning, the promoter has the vision and the public has the money. At the end, the promoter has the money and the public has the vision."

Source: <www.CartoonStock.com>.

Agribusiness investments

Agribusiness investments include forestry and horticultural projects. Unfortunately, over recent times, investing in these types of investments has received a bad reputation. The much-publicised collapses of Timbercorp and Great Southern in the GFC have severely dented investor confidence in this type of alternative investment. The agribusiness investment sector has gone from a position where there were many projects to invest in, to a point where now there are virtually no projects available.

Personal note

Agribusiness investments is another area of investing where I can draw on personal experience. Over the years I have invested in 25-year pine projects, 12-year blue gum projects and two 25-year horticultural projects.

I have in one case definitely lost my investment, but with the others I'm still hopeful of receiving a return. I have joint ventured the two horticultural projects with my self managed super fund in the expectation of a regular income being generated from the sale of the crops that will produce cash to help fund my retirement income.

Despite the problems that agribusiness continues to experience, I still believe there is a place for this type of investment. Its future will depend on a more sustainable investment model being developed. Unfortunately for investors, managed investments schemes, the vehicle used for agribusiness investments, were hijacked by the commission-driven financial planning industry. This was a case of the financial planner tail wagging the managed investment scheme agribusiness industry dog. Many advisers, driven by the lure of 10 per cent commissions, sold these investments more on the tax reduction benefits than on investment returns and demanded that projects be structured in a way that made them unsustainable: so that the advisers' commissions could be maximised in the year investors entered the investment, financial planners demanded projects with large upfront tax-deductible costs and no ongoing maintenance fees.

Agribusiness as an investment going forward will only work if proper business and financial principles are applied. This means that, in addition to an initial large investment being required to establish the project, investors also have a financial commitment to fund the ongoing maintenance and business costs of the project. This is the way horticultural agribusiness projects, as opposed to forestry projects, are structured, and that is the reason why in many cases they have a better chance of surviving in the long term.

One of the biggest impediments to an investment in forestry projects is how long it takes for income to be produced. For some projects, such as pine tree and mahogany plantations, the main harvest proceeds are not produced until after 20 years. This can make this sort of investment useful for someone who wants to retire before they have reached retirement age and can access their superannuation.

The risks to consider before investing in the agribusiness sector are market, environment, fire and manager performance. The fire risk in most cases is extremely well managed by project managers, and insurance can be taken out to protect the grower.

The recent drought is a great example of the environmental risk faced by anyone in the agricultural sector. Investors can reduce this risk by investing in a number of projects located in different geographic and climatic regions.

The market risk is real, but this has been reduced due to the increasing demand that comes from growing populations around the world, and the diminishing land area being used for agriculture and timber projects.

The task of choosing a company to manage an agribusiness investment was once difficult, due to the large number of projects and managers available. The task is just as hard now, but that is because there are so few projects and managers. The best criterion to use when picking a management company is choose one that comes from an agriculture or growing background rather than a funds management background. This need is demonstrated even more clearly by the two celebrated collapses in the agribusiness managed investment scheme area: Great Southern and Timbercorp were primarily fund managers rather than growers.

If a decision is made to invest in the alternative asset class, you need careful assessment and to get professional advice. If you are offered a chance to invest in something that doesn't make sense, if there is little or no transparency about the activities of the fund manager, or you can't work out exactly how a profit is made, do not invest.

Getting the balance right

Funding your retirement is not just about doing one thing right: it is about doing a series of things throughout your life, which can be thought of as being split into two distinct phases. The first is the accumulation phase, when the object is to accumulate the amount of retirement investment assets required to produce the income you need in retirement. The second is the retirement, or drawdown, phase when you depend on your investment assets to produce both income and capital growth to continue to provide your desired lifestyle. Both phases depend on your deciding the income you need to support your lifestyle and having the discipline to live within your budget. The question of discipline becomes critical in the retirement phase if you want to ensure your retirement assets will outlive you or last at least until you die, or if you want to leave something for your children.

As the GFC showed, many people, even though they had accumulated what they regarded as sufficient investment assets to fund their retirement, could still face dire consequences if they ignored another important ingredient of wealth protection. This important ingredient is balancing your investments across the different asset classes.

Traditionally the financial planning industry has model portfolios that allocate investments across the main asset sectors, according to a person's tolerance of risk. This risk is all about how worried someone is about losing their money in an investment. The higher the concern about losing money, in other words the lower the tolerance to risk, the greater the percentage invested in defensive assets such as term deposits.

I prefer to allocate investments across the different asset sectors based on the length of time the person will hold the investments and the stage that an individual is at in their investing life. Whatever method is followed, a balance needs to be maintained across the different asset classes.

The main objectives in asset allocation should be to:

- take advantage of capital appreciation that comes from growth assets
- generate enough income to either draw down for living expenses or accumulate for growth and future expenses
- ensure that in retirement you are not forced to sell assets to meet lifestyle costs

- provide a methodology to rebalance the portfolio, by selling an asset class when it becomes overvalued and buying an asset class that has become undervalued in a way that is not based on emotion such as fear in falling markets and excitement in rising markets.

Five asset allocation models

In the following sections I outline five main model asset allocation portfolios designed for investors of different ages. In chapter 6, I listed the various wealth creation strategies based on the age of the person and the stage they were in during their financial life. The five model asset allocations apply to different life stages, and sometimes to more than one stage. They are also linked to people's risk tolerance, no matter what stage of life they are at. These are prudent suggestions only—the percentage of your assets actually allocated to each class is a very personal decision.

Each of the model portfolios has a target allocation, which is the holding that would apply when market conditions are settled. Upper and lower ranges are also suggested, to allow some choice when investment markets are unsettled. I have included an allocation to international fixed interest, but I have not personally invested in this sector as income returns have been very low and the risks associated with market valuations and currency fluctuations make it less attractive.

In the models, the closer you are to retirement phase, the more the cash component increases. This has been done to ensure there will be sufficient cash to fund your cost of living without your having to sell investments, and also to recognise that there are times when markets become over-heated, and when this occurs, it is prudent to increase cash holdings to take advantage of market corrections or crashes.

I am not recommending holding all your assets in cash, as this is like trying to time the markets, which is a strategy fraught with danger.

By deciding which asset allocation best suits you, and having the discipline and courage to stick with it, will assist you to, again as Warren Buffett put it, 'profit from folly rather than participate in it'.

Asset allocation for experienced investors and the young

Asset allocation for experienced investors and the young applies to stages 1 and 2 of a person's financial life as described in chapter 6. This allocation can also apply to experienced investors who are not scared of the risks associated with the more volatile investments. It applies when there is a long time before the investment assets will be needed for retirement purposes — at least 25 years. Although the value of these investments will fall at times, because amounts are being invested regularly, investors gain the advantage of dollar cost averaging. The model asset allocation portfolio for experienced investors and the young is shown in table 8.2.

Table 8.2: model asset allocation for experienced investors and the young

Asset class	Target allocation (%)	Upper and lower ranges (%)
Australian equities	55	40–55
International equities	30	25–35
Property	5	5–15
Australian fixed interest	4	0–10
International fixed interest	0	0–5
Cash	1	0–3
Alternatives	5	0–10
Total	**100**	

Asset allocation for the middle stages of life

This asset allocation applies to someone in stage 3 of their financial life. The value of their investment assets is starting to increase and so the allocation to the less volatile sectors increases. There are still at least 20 years to go until retirement and the long-term investing view still applies. The model asset allocation portfolio for the middle stages of life is shown in table 8.3.

Table 8.3: model asset allocation for the middle stages of life

Asset class	Target allocation (%)	Upper and lower ranges (%)
Australian equities	45	40–55
International equities	30	25–35
Property	13	5–15
Australian fixed interest	5	0–10
International fixed interest	0	0–5
Cash	2	0–3
Alternatives	5	0–10
Total	**100**	

Asset allocation for those closer to retirement and for anyone who wants a well-balanced portfolio

This model portfolio seeks to maintain a balance across the various asset classes, as shown in table 8.4 (overleaf). It is more applicable to people in stages 4 and 5 of their financial lives and for anyone who prefers to take a balanced view of investing. It is also applicable for someone in retirement, as it provides a good balance between income-producing investments and investments held for growth. The time horizon is between five years and 50 years.

Table 8.4: model asset allocation for people close to retirement and those who want a well-balanced portfolio

Asset class	Target allocation (%)	Upper and lower ranges (%)
Australian equities	30	25–35
International equities	10	5–15
Property	25	15–30
Australian fixed interest	20	15–25
International fixed interest	5	0–10
Cash	5	3–50
Alternatives	5	0–10
Total	**100**	

Asset allocation for those in retirement and the risk averse

This model portfolio applies to people who would have sleepless nights worrying about their investments if they took too much risk, and for people who have been in retirement for some time. It recognises the importance of having growth assets to protect investors against the impact of inflation, but also takes account of the importance of preserving capital and having sufficient cash to fund living expenses, as shown in table 8.5.

Table 8.5: model asset allocation for those in retirement and the risk averse

Asset class	Target allocation (%)	Upper and lower ranges (%)
Australian equities	20	10–30
International equities	5	0–10
Property	25	20–30
Australian fixed interest	35	25–40
International fixed interest	5	0–10
Cash	10	5–80
Alternatives	0	0
Total	**100**	

*Asset allocation for the later stages of life
and the very conservative*

This model applies to someone in the later stages of their life, and people who cannot stand investment risk at all. This group have a short-term investment horizon of no more than three years and are focused on income and not capital growth. The model asset allocation portfolio for this group is shown in table 8.6.

Table 8.6: model asset allocation for the later stages of life and the very conservative

Asset class	Target allocation (%)	Upper and lower ranges (%)
Australian equities	5	0–10
International equities	0	0
Property	15	10–20
Australian fixed interest	45	20–50
Cash	35	10–100
Alternatives	0	0
Total	**100**	

Rebalancing

Having worked out which asset allocation best fits your stage in life and tolerance to investment risk, the job does not finish there. In stages 1 and 2 of your financial life, where you have a high percentage invested in growth assets, the amount you have in cash needs to be reviewed. This is particularly the case if you are salary sacrificing money into superannuation. Some superannuation funds will allocate super contributions across your chosen asset allocation, while others will deposit the super contributions into your cash account in the superannuation fund. In this case a transfer should be done from cash into the other asset classes to rebalance your superannuation account.

In the later stages of your financial life where you are starting to have a more balanced distribution across the different asset classes, it is more important to regularly rebalance your total investment portfolio. This is because the percentage of each asset class in your total portfolio can fall outside the desired holding range. This can occur, for instance, when one asset class has a major increase in value or has a major decrease in value. It can also happen as a result of income or super contributions going into cash, which means it is building up above the target holding percentage.

By taking the time to work out what your target holdings will be, and applying a disciplined approach to regularly rebalancing your portfolio, you stand a better chance of not suffering huge investment losses while also profiting from the inevitable chaos of the investment markets. If there is one constant in investment markets it is the inevitable boom and bust cycle that has been with us for centuries.

By regularly rebalancing your portfolio you should find that you are selling investments at a profit, as a result of their having increased in value and being worth more in your portfolio than your maximum allocation to that asset class should be. You should also increase your investments in the asset classes that have either dropped in value or have been stagnant, and therefore provide great potential for growth in the future.

When you are in retirement, rebalancing your portfolio at least once a year not only makes investment sense, it can also be vital if you want to protect the value of your retirement assets. You need to ensure that there are sufficient cash holdings, after conservatively estimating the income the investments will earn over the next 12 months, to fund the income you need in retirement.

Personal note

When conducting reviews for clients who are in pension mode, I take a conservative approach to the amount of cash they should hold at the start of each financial year. I usually have at least half of that year's annual income requirement in cash. This ensures that investments should not need to be sold during the year to fund the retirement income. This is because the investment income earned during the year, when added to the starting value of cash, should ensure there is always sufficient cash to pay the pension.

In addition, both for people in retirement and the accumulation stage, I prefer to have income from the various investments they hold paid into the cash account. This means if I'm reviewing a client's portfolio once a year, I can use the cash holding to assist with rebalancing and reduce the need to sell investments to achieve the desired asset mix.

Conclusion

In finishing this chapter I would like to leave you with two quotations that go right to the heart of the fact that nearly all asset classes go through turmoil at some point or another, and that there is a direct link between risk and return. The first is from William J Bernstein's book *The Four Pillars of Investing*: 'Do not expect high returns without high risk. Do not expect safety without corresponding low returns.

Further, when the political and economic outlook is the brightest, returns are the lowest. And it is when things look the darkest that returns are the highest.'

The second is attributed to the novelist Graham Greene, who makes the same point in a slightly different way: 'In Italy for thirty years under the Borgias they had warfare, terror, murder and bloodshed, but they produced Michelangelo, Leonardo da Vinci and the Renaissance. In Switzerland they had brotherly love and five hundred years of democracy and peace. What did they produce? The cuckoo clock.'

CHAPTER 9

The facts and myths about property investment

When it comes to investing in real estate Australians can't seem to get enough. In fact with much of Australia's real estate not providing good investment opportunities owing to increases in the value over recent years, some people are even looking at investing in the depressed US real estate market.

Investing in property can bring many rewards. Where gearing is involved, the losses can help reduce income tax. This benefit can, however, come at the cost of a significant drain on cash flow, depending on the individual's tax rate and what type of property has been purchased.

The choices for investing in direct property are between buying a new property or one that is established, and choosing either commercial premises or a domestic property. Each choice offers different opportunities and tax benefits. When it comes to residential property most of the gain is expected to come from capital growth.

The problem is that not everybody is making the level of return that they think they are from property. For example, if a property doubles in value over 10 years, it has not had a 100 per cent return; in fact it has made only a 7 per cent compounded return over that period.

It is also important to understand that there are two types of property investments. The first is a lifestyle property investment and the second is a financial property investment. A lifestyle property investment is when someone buys property more for lifestyle reasons than for wealth creation. In this case matters of the heart tend to outweigh financial facts and logic. Financial property investment, however, is all about wealth creation and so decisions here should be based on what produces the best return and not what looks nice. Investing in property, rather than being simple, is in fact complicated, which is borne out by the number of choices a person has. These include whether to:

- buy new residential property
- buy an established residential property
- buy property off the plan from a developer
- buy property to subdivide
- knock down an existing property and rebuild
- buy a house
- buy a unit
- buy a flat
- buy an apartment.

Residential property can be useful from a negative gearing tax perspective, which helps divert income to a growth asset and provides a tax benefit along the way, but it traditionally produces a very low income return. Because of this, a residential property can make sense while you're in wealth accumulation phase, but it can cause serious problems when you have retired.

Finding the right property: location, location, location

Whether you are investing in property or shares, the best way I know of maximising your potential capital growth is to buy something that is undervalued. Several well-known sayings apply when it comes to investing in property.

The first is the three things that maximise the potential for making a profit from property are location, location, location. Sometimes people wanting to invest in property are drawn to something that is cheap, without properly considering the reason for its low price. Sometimes property is cheap because of its location. Just like all assets where a market exists, there is a direct link between supply and demand. Highly attractive locations, such as inner-city areas and the more salubrious suburbs, often experience greater demand than can be supplied, so these areas are more expensive and are often the first to rise in value after a real estate slump. Conversely, property in locations that are less desirable, whether that is because of their remoteness or the general condition of the properties in the surrounding suburbs, often have more people wanting to move out of the area then there are wanting to buy in. This is the reason why they are cheap, and they will probably remain cheap.

The second saying is 'always buy the worst house in the best street'. This goes to the heart of the first saying. This means you need to do your research and work out what areas are regarded as more desirable than others. You need to get a feel for what the market value of the better presented properties are, and then try to find a property that is the sow's ear that can be turned into a silk purse. For example, a beautifully presented house that has been renovated and appeals immediately to potential buyers will more than likely be relatively expensive. A house that has been rented out for several years, has a garden in a distressed state, shows signs of wear and tear and bad colour schemes, and little or no renovations or improvements made recently, could represent good value if it is in the right location.

Before committing to a property that is the worst house in the best street, get a building surveyor's report. Without this you cannot be sure that the house is sound and that expensive major structural works won't need to be carried out. You should then obtain estimates of what it will take to improve the house to bring it into a condition where it will be the equal of the other homes in that location. At this point you should be able to do your sums on what you believe you can pay for the property, and how much it will cost to improve and renovate it, and assess the potential for capital growth when its price is compared with those for other properties that have been improved.

There is a direct link between the potential capital growth to be made from property and the amount of effort and work put into properly researching the investment. The other important thing to remove from the decision to buy an investment property is emotion, unless the property will have a dual investment and lifestyle purpose, such as a holiday home. In this situation the heart can dictate the location, but at least the head can try to make sure you don't pay too much.

Personal note

A good example of a financial lifestyle investment is a real estate purchase my wife and I made in the late 1990s. We had retired friends who owned a unit on the Gold Coast.

They rented it out on a holiday letting basis during the summer months, which is the peak demand season for locals, and in the cold Melbourne winter moved north to live in the sunshine for several months.

As my own retirement was not that far away, and because the real estate market on the Gold Coast had been in a slump for several years, we thought it would make sense to buy a property up there that we could also enjoy in our retirement and rent out in the meantime.

By buying when we had the income to support the negative cash flow from the purchase costs and rent, and at a time when the market was flat, it made good investment sense and offered a chance of an improved lifestyle in retirement.

This decision happened to coincide with my attending a conference on the Gold Coast. While I was trapped inside a dark auditorium listening to numerous speakers, my wife contacted several local real estate agents and looked at what was available. We had originally set a budget of approximately $130 000 to buy a unit.

After four or five days of my conferencing, I was finally able to go through the list of possible investment options that my wife had come up with. It came down to a choice between an older unit in the suburb of Surfers Paradise that fitted our original budget, or a newer unit in the more desirable suburb of Main Beach, which cost $155 000.

Recognising that the potential for capital gain was greater in Main Beach, and that the extra financing costs would amount to only about $37 a week, we made the decision to buy the unit there. Another fact that convinced us to buy this unit was that when the developers had sold the unit about five years before, it had cost the original purchaser $175 000.

Financing the purchase

Just as it pays to do your research when buying a property it also pays to do the research when looking for finance. In fact, this research is sometimes best done even before the property is found. That means you will know how much you can borrow based on other security you may be offering and your ability to repay the loan, so you can sometimes pick up a property cheaper by making an unconditional offer for a lower price.

Following the golden rule of borrowing, which, if you have forgotten, is pay cash for private and borrow for investment, you should finance the investment property with an interest-only loan. It can also make sense to pay a slightly higher interest rate for a more flexible type of loan, such as a line of credit, for an investment property. These loans establish an initial borrowing limit that can be greater than the purchase price. This makes it possible to finance some or all of the purchase costs.

Lines of credit can also mean that, where you have a private loan, such as a home mortgage, you don't make interest payments on the investment loan for a period. This will allow you to maximise your repayments on the non–tax deductible private loan and reduce it as much as possible as quickly as possible. To put this into context, someone on the 31.5 per cent tax rate must earn $10 000 to make a principal repayment off a loan of $6850. It therefore does not make sense where there is a private loan and an investment loan to use this valuable cash resource to reduce the investment loan. Even though the total net asset position is the same, the amount of tax-deductible interest has been reduced and the negative gearing tax benefit is also reduced.

Finding an agent or renting it yourself

Most people who invest in domestic property, unless they are running it as a business and have many properties, tend to use a real estate agent to manage the rental activities. This includes finding appropriate tenants, collecting the rent, dealing with tenant problems, and regularly inspecting the property to ensure the tenants are looking after it.

Finding an agent that does all of these things to a reasonable standard for a reasonable cost should be easy — the problem is it's not. Just as there are many horror stories about bad tenants — a favourite of mine is the tenant who disassembled his car engine in the lounge room of his rented property — there are just as many horror stories about agents. If you are going to use an agent check around as to what other agents are charging for their services and make sure you know exactly what is provided. This includes the number of times the agent will visit the property to check on its condition.

The alternative to using an agent is managing the rental property yourself. This does require a lot more work from you as the investor, but it will save you the real estate management fees and provide a better result, as you will tend to make sure that the tenants are looking after the property. For someone with the time to take on the property management tasks this can be combined with the maintenance of the property and the garden. When you don't have the time or the inclination to manage the property yourself it does make sense to have it managed by a professional.

Maximising your rental property tax deductions

The impact on an investor's cash flow of deductible costs depends on their type. Some costs are deductible in the year they are paid, such as rates and agent's fees. For other costs, only a portion is deductible in the year in which they are paid. Furniture, fixtures and fittings are examples of costs that are not fully deductible in the year they are purchased, because they will be written off over their estimated useful life. Some costs can only be used to decrease a capital gain when the property is sold.

One cost, depending on when the property was constructed, delivers a tax deduction over the period it is owned and produces income. This is the cost of the building itself. There have been many changes to the way construction costs can be written off over the years. These changes have resulted in different annual write-off rates that depend on the date construction commenced and the type of property. In all cases, the rate of write off is done under the prime cost or straight-line depreciation method. Both methods result in an annual amount that does not change each year.

For commercial properties (such as shops, offices and factories) where construction commenced between 21 July 1982 and 19 July 1985 the annual write off is 2.5 per cent. For those properties and income-producing residential properties where construction commenced between 19 July 1985 and 15 September 1987, the annual write off is 4 per cent.

For most income-producing properties where construction commenced after 15 September 1987 the annual write off remains unchanged at 2.5 per cent. The exceptions to this are manufacturing properties and short-term traveller accommodation. Both of these types of properties can be written off at 4 per cent where construction commenced after 26 February 1992.

The ability to claim the tax deduction for construction costs is not limited to the original owner. The annual tax deduction passes from one owner to the next as long as the property is used to produce assessable income. In some cases the vendor of the property will provide the amount that can be claimed as a tax deduction. This amount is often a selling point for properties purchased from developers. In this case the purchaser is given a depreciation schedule that details all costs that can be written off, split into fixtures and fittings, and construction costs. Where the vendor does not provide the details of the annual deductible amounts, this information can still be obtained, because quantity surveyors in every Australian capital city specialise in providing this information. Investors wanting to maximise their annual property deductions realise the cost of getting a quantity surveyor's depreciation report is often outweighed by the increased tax deduction and refund.

If you have a rental property and have not had a depreciation schedule prepared all is not lost. You can get a quantity surveyor to prepare one and, as well as including the tax deduction in your next tax return, you can also go back and increase the tax deduction for up to two years.

Buying from a developer

I personally don't recommend buying property from developers. This is because there are often so many layers of cost included in these properties, such as marketing and selling costs, that investors end up paying a lot more than the true market value. (The unit I bought on the Gold Coast is a great example of that.) The only time that this doesn't happen is if you are buying from a developer during a depressed property market before the start of the next property boom cycle.

And not all property developers are created equal. Some develop properties and sell them for a reasonable price, but others are a lot less scrupulous. There have been numerous examples over the years of property developers colluding with valuers and financiers to the detriment of investors. In these cases people paid inflated values for properties financed 100 per cent by the tame financier. To entice purchasers to invest in the overpriced real estate, in some cases rental guarantees are also provided.

"Brick is overrated. Let me show you something in sticks or straw."

Source: <www.CartoonStock.com>.

The problem for an investor if you buy from one of these developers is that at the first signs of trouble the owners of the development company walk away with huge profits.

This often leaves a two-dollar company that is unable to pay the rental guarantees. Investors can then find themselves stuck with a property that does not produce income and has a market value well below the total owing on the loan.

If for some reason the property you want to buy can only be bought through a developer, you can take action to make sure you're not paying too much. Most experienced quantity surveyors should be able to provide an estimate of the cost of the structure after they have been provided with all of the specifications and relevant details of the property being purchased. Once you know roughly how much the building costs, you can calculate how much you are paying for your share of the location and the other add-on costs, such as marketing and selling commissions. It is also worthwhile to look at real estate listings for similar established properties in the area to gauge whether you are getting good value or paying too much.

If a property developer offers to fly you interstate to show you the properties they have for sale, run a mile. In this situation I can guarantee that you will be confronted with high-pressure sales techniques, and the marketing and selling costs will make it very difficult for you to realise a capital gain if you buy a property in this situation.

Purchasing in a different state

Not all of the best real estate opportunities are in the area where you live. Sometimes they can be several hours drive away or even interstate. The further a rental property is from where you live the harder it can be to manage the investment. In these cases a professional property manager must be used.

This is another example of where the amount of research and work that goes into finding the property and the managers really pays off. Unfortunately, when it comes to purchasing units or flats, it can often be limited to using the onsite managers of the property.

Tax traps and myths

There are many myths about what tax advantages come with a property investment. Where an investor does not understand the taxation rules, and the investor is audited, the resulting tax penalties can eat up any investment benefits.

Travel costs

One of the first tax myths of property investment relates to claiming travel costs. This is especially the case for interstate property ownership. There is a general misconception that all costs associated with visiting a rental property are tax deductible, such as airfares, accommodation and incidentals. Nothing could be further from the truth.

The amount that can be claimed for travel expenses is determined by how much time is spent related to the rental property. If you had a Queensland rental property and flew up there, stayed a week, and spent an hour inspecting the property, very little of the travel costs would be tax deductible. If, on the other hand you spent a week arranging repairs, carrying out some repairs yourself, visiting the agent, buying furniture, and generally spent nearly all of your time on property matters, the whole of the travel costs would be tax deductible.

Motor vehicle travel costs are also deductible for properties, but if the travel involves only driving past the property it would be hard to justify a claim. If the trip relates to driving to the property and getting out to collect rent, inspect the property when a tenant leaves or see if they are looking after the property, or mowing the grass and carrying out repairs, a claim could be made for the travel. In most cases the kilometre basis is the best method to use as it is not feasible for an investor with one property to keep a logbook, and they would not normally do more than 5000 kilometres a year on rental property activities.

The tax deductibility of interest

Another tax myth of property investing is the tax deductibility of interest on loans. The property used as security for a loan does not dictate whether the interest is tax deductible: it is the purpose for which the funds have been borrowed. If the purpose of a loan is to purchase a home, rather than an investment property, the interest on the loan will not be tax deductible.

A situation where this occurs most commonly is when a decision is made to purchase a new home but keep the old home as a rental property. Often the loan to purchase the original home has been almost repaid and there is a lot of equity in the property. Where a new loan is taken out using that equity, and the funds are used to purchase the new home, the interest is not tax deductible.

From a tax point of view, it makes a lot more sense to sell the original home, make a tax-free capital gain on the sale, use the funds to purchase the new home, making this loan as small as possible, then find a new property to purchase as an investment.

Apportionment of costs

Where a property has two purposes, such as a rental property used for private purposes, a tax deduction for all the costs related to that property cannot be claimed. An example of this would be a seaside property that is used by the owners and their friends at no cost. In this situation the costs of that property must be apportioned between the private use and the investment use.

A reasonable way of doing this is on a time basis. If a holiday home is available for rent for 52 weeks of the year, and is not used by the owners unless they are doing the gardening or maintenance on the property, all the cost should be tax deductible. If, on the other hand, a holiday home is used by the owner for two out of the 10 weeks that it could normally be rented out, 20 per cent of the property's costs, including interest, could not be claimed as a tax deduction. If the ATO can show that the owners of the property had not made every possible effort to rent it out, and used it themselves, the whole of property could be regarded as personal and private, and nothing would be deductible.

Legal fees and borrowing costs

When a property is purchased there will usually be conveyancing and other costs related to transferring the property into the name of the investor. In addition, when a loan is taken out to purchase an investment property an establishment fee is often paid. Legal costs related to the purchase of the property must be added to the purchase cost and can be used to decrease any future capital gain. However, legal fees related to preparing new leases, taking legal action for recovery of rent, and anything else related to the rent-producing activities, will be tax deductible in the year they are paid.

Borrowing costs are not tax deductible fully in the year they are incurred. Instead borrowing costs of more than $100 are deductible over the period of the loan, or over a period of five years, whichever is less. For example, a 25-year principal and interest loan with a $500 establishment fee results in annual deductible borrowing costs of $100. A line of credit facility costing $900 that runs for three years results in an annual borrowing cost deduction of $300.

Repairs

One tax myth of property investing is that all amounts spent on repairing a property are tax deductible. A tax deduction can only be claimed for repairs to a rental property, not for improvements.

Generally, for something to qualify as a repair all the asset can't be replaced. When the whole asset is replaced, such as a stove, this will more than likely be classed as an improvement. An example of a repair is where part of a roof is replaced because of storm damage. Where an entire roof is replaced, this will be in most cases an improvement. Improvements are also work that makes the condition of an asset better than it was when purchased.

Repairs carried out after purchasing a property to get it into a condition where it can be rented are not tax deductible because they are classed as improvements. Where a property has been rented for some time, and work is carried out such as painting to repair damage while the property was rented, the cost will be tax deductible.

Purchase costs

The costs associated with finding and buying a property are not tax deductible. Most of the costs related to the purchase of the property are included when calculating whether a capital gain or loss is made on the sale of the property.

One cost that is not tax deductible, either against rent or as a purchase cost, is travel to find a property to purchase. This means that, despite what property developers may tell you, the cost of travelling somewhere to find a property to purchase is a general cost and it cannot be included as a cost of the property, which means that it is effectively lost money.

Purchase costs that can't be claimed as a deduction against rental income but form part of the capital cost include:

- fees paid to a surveyor, valuer, auctioneer, broker, agent, consultant or lawyer
- costs of transfer
- stamp duty or other similar duty
- costs of advertising or marketing when selling
- costs relating to the making of any valuation or apportionment to determine your capital gain or capital loss
- search fees relating to an asset
- the cost of a conveyancing kit.

The tax office website has some excellent information about what you can and can't claim when it comes to rental properties. Go to <www.ato.gov.au> and type 'rental properties' into the search field.

Calculating your capital gain on a property

There is a strict sequence that must be followed when calculating the assessable portion of a capital gain. These steps are as follows:

1 the profit or loss on sale is calculated by deducting all costs of the asset sold from net sale proceeds

2 capital losses made on the sale of assets in the current year are deducted

3 capital losses carried forward from previous years are deducted

4 if the asset was held for more than 12 months, the gain is reduced by the general 50 per cent discount

5 the resulting gain is then included as assessable income.

Other discounts apply if the person selling the asset is classed as a small business owner. Where losses have been made on other activities during the year the gain is made, such as a rental property loss, this loss and tax losses carried forward from previous years also reduce the amount of taxable capital gain.

Conclusion

An investment property can be an extremely worthwhile investment. In addition to diverting income for an investment purpose to help fund your retirement, above-average returns can be achieved provided you avoid the traps and mistakes of property investment described here.

This chapter has aimed to provide you with information to help you maximise your returns from a property investment. You should, however, also seek further professional advice from both real estate and tax experts to make sure you achieve the best result.

CHAPTER 10

Getting the right advice

In this chapter I am, to use the immortal words of politician Don Chipp, trying to 'keep the bastards honest'. An unfortunate fact of the financial planning industry, both here and overseas, has been that many of the advisers have been more focused on maximising their commission income than on the financial wellbeing and future of their clients.

One of the main reasons I started providing wealth creation advice was seeing how badly my clients were being ripped off. This included clients:

- being signed up for incredibly expensive super-annuation funds that resulted in the sales agent earning maximum commissions that the clients paid for with exorbitant administration fees and under-performing investments
- being sold investment properties in supposedly growth areas of Queensland that, in fact, only increased the net income of the developer and the salesperson
- being talked into an asset allocation for their super fund that was predominantly allocated to the sharemarket when the client was nearing retirement

- being sold managed investments held in expensive administration and wrap platforms when the client had sufficient funds and expertise to either invest directly in the share market or in wholesale managed investments.

Two main factors have contributed to the poor quality of advice given to Australians over the years. The first is that most so-called advisers earn their income as commissions on the products they sell rather than the advice they give. The second is that financial institutions, such as banks and insurance companies—the companies that make their income from putting together and maintaining the different investment products—also own companies that provide advice to investors.

Commission versus fee for service

There is thankfully a light at the end of the tunnel, which will increase the chance of investors receiving investment advice they can rely on. This is the news that the government intends to introduce legislation to ban commissions. In April 2010 the federal Labor government announced that it would ban financial planners charging commission-based fees from 1 July 2012. This news, as you would expect, caused a great deal of concern among traditional financial planners, who tried to make a case for investors being worse off as a result.

One of the main reasons given for retaining commissions was that a fee-for-service model would mean low-income earners could not afford to get advice. This is because under fee for service a client pays, and knows they are paying, for the service they are receiving. Under a commission situation the client pays much more but is often blissfully unaware of the true cost of the supposed advice.

This criticism put forward by the commission-driven advisers is not valid for two reasons. First, in many cases the commissions charged to a low-income earner over the life of their investment—a fact they are often unaware of—ends up costing them dearly. Second, the reforms will allow advice fees to be paid out of financial products, such as managed investments and superannuation accounts.

This argument also ignores the main reason why the measure must be adopted. For too long investors have sought wealth creation advice and instead have been sold product. When there is a direct link between advice and commissions this will always occur.

At the time of writing, the legislation to ban commissions had not yet been introduced into parliament. Even if the changes do not come into effect, investors can improve their chances of getting strategy-based, instead of product-based, advice by being aware of how the financial advice industry works.

At present many financial advisers work for companies, such as banks and insurance companies, that expect the adviser to be a distribution channel for their products. This means when you get advice from one of these advisers you are mainly getting product-based advice. It is not hard to find examples of this. In fact some bank tellers are rewarded for referring customers with large amounts in accounts to the financial planner associated with the bank. And if you get advice from a financial planner who works for one of the large insurance companies, you will end up with their insurance policies and the financial products managed by one of the companies the insurance company owns.

The same applies to getting financial advice from specialist financial advisers, such as stockbrokers and real estate agents. In these cases, the advice given will be slanted toward the product they sell, rather than what is best for the person seeking the advice.

Getting the best advice

In addition to being aware of where your advice comes from, you can also ask several questions to ensure you get the best advice. These are:

- Is the fee you charge for the advice and the placing of investments on my behalf based on the complexity of the issues and the time it takes rather than as a percentage of the amount invested?
- Do you split your advice between strategic advice and product advice?
- Do you provide ongoing advice for a fee instead of charging a percentage of the amount invested?
- Are you able to provide advice on direct investments or are you limited to advising on managed investments that pay trails and commissions?

If the answer to any of these questions is 'no', you need to look for another adviser.

One way of keeping the cost of advice down is to know what you want. This means if you don't want a full retirement plan, but have several superannuation funds and want advice on consolidating your super and using salary sacrifice, ask for specific advice in this area.

This book is meant to help you in two ways when it comes to getting advice. First, it aims to help you gain an understanding of the wealth creation process, and the different options you have for funding your retirement, so you can critically assess the financial advice you receive. Second, as the cost of advice should be based on the complexities of the issues and the length of time it takes to do the work, by following the steps set out in chapter 2, and thinking about what strategies may be suitable for you as were outlined in chapter 6, less work will be required by the person you seek advice from because you will already have been able to make some decisions about where you need help.

"I'm a little concerned about my financial advisor. He said to keep 60% in equities, 25% in bonds, and 25% in cash."

Source: <www.CartoonStock.com>.

Instead of doing everything for you, all the adviser needs to do is:

- confirm your income, expenses, assets and liabilities
- review your financial and retirement goals
- assess the suitability of the strategies you have chosen and suggest alternative or additional strategies
- analyse all of your information and strategies, and prepare projections of what your financial and tax benefits will be
- confirm that you will be able to fund your retirement.

CHAPTER 11

Questions and answers

The following questions and answers are a selection of those sent in by readers of my superannuation and investing columns that appear in Melbourne's *The Age*, *The Sydney Morning Herald* and other Fairfax publications, some in the print version and others only in the online versions.

Rental properties: deductible rental loss or private arrangement?

Q I have an investment property that I allowed my mother to live in rent-free while she was in Melbourne receiving treatment for cancer. Since then I have had a friend renting my property. There is no contract and no real estate agents are involved, and she is paying a lot less than my mortgage payments. Can I still regard the property as negatively geared?

A For a property to be regarded as negatively geared the property must be used for an investment purpose and not a private one. For the time your mother was living in the property it was used for a private purpose, and therefore the negative gearing loss for this period is not deductible.

With the property now rented to your friend you could claim the negative gearing loss if you can show that the rent she pays is commercial. The amount could be slightly below the full market rent, to take account of the saving you receive by not having an agent, but it could not be significantly less. If the rent were significantly less, the property would be regarded as still being used for private purposes.

Q My husband and I are thinking about purchasing a holiday home and at the same time want to rent it out as a holiday let to generate some income during the summer months. We also want to maintain it as owner-occupied so that over time we will not have to incur capital gains tax if we end up selling the property. We would appreciate it if you could advise if that is workable and what would be the tax guidelines for such a purchase.

A The first problem to address is your belief that you may be able to make a tax-free capital gain on the sale of the property. The exemption from capital gains tax applies only to a person's principal place of residence. This means that if you already have a home, and the new property will purely be a holiday home that is rented, you will pay capital gains tax on any profit you make when it is sold.

In addition, you will be able to claim a tax deduction only for the investment use of the property. This means that if the property is only available for rent for six out of 52 weeks of the year, you can only claim 8.67 per cent of the property's costs, including interest and rates.

Capital gains tax and death

Q Up to 1974 two of my great aunts jointly owned and lived in a house in inner city Perth. In 1974 one aunt died and left me her half share in the house. The other aunt continued to live in the house until 1989, and then she moved to an old people's home. The house remained empty. She died in 1995 and left me her half share of the house. If I sell the property what will I pay capital gains tax on?

A The amount of capital gains tax payable when an inherited asset is sold depends on when the original owner purchased it, and when the seller inherited it. Where an asset was purchased by the deceased before 20 September 1985 the cost of the asset for tax purposes is the value at the date of death. For assets purchased by the deceased after September 1985, the cost is that paid by the deceased.

Assets inherited before September 1985 will not be assessed for capital gains taxed when sold. For assets inherited after that date, capital gains tax is payable on the excess of the selling proceeds over the cost.

The exception to this is where a principal place of residence is inherited. If the house meets all the exemption conditions, the former principal place of residence can be sold and no tax is payable on the gain if the settlement takes place within two years of the deceased's death.

In your situation half the house was inherited by you before September 1985 and no tax will be payable on half the gain. For the other half, you will need to get a valuation of the house at the date of death of your aunt in 1995. As you will be selling the house more than two years after she died, tax will be payable.

The amount of capital gains tax payable is calculated by deducting half the value of the house in 1995 from half the net proceeds you receive. If there have been costs related to the house that were not tax deductible since 1995, such as renovations or other costs if the property was not rented, these can be added to the 1995 value.

Tax will be payable by you, at your relevant marginal rate of tax, on half of the gain you make. Given that this gain will more than likely be substantial, you should seek professional advice to see if there are any steps you can take to reduce your amount of tax payable.

Q I am 69 years old, on a pension and live with my 10-year-old son. What is the best way to leave him our residence without or with minimum tax payable? What is the best way to leave him my other assets with minimum tax payable?

A If your son inherits your home and continues living in it he will not pay any tax when it is sold. This is because the property will have been a principal place of residence at all times during its ownership.

With regard to your other assets you should consider, while your son is under 18, the formation of a testamentary trust that will be set up upon your death. With such a trust, if you die before he turns 18, any income produced by those assets will be taxed as if he was an adult. If you didn't set up a testamentary trust, as a minor, he would have to pay punitive rates of tax.

Q I have been led to believe that capital gains tax is payable on shares inherited from a parent only in the event they are sold. My mother is 96, in aged care, and has a very large parcel of Commonwealth Bank shares that cost about $10 each when they were purchased in 1986. When I inherit them what will be my cost? It is my understanding that no tax would be payable until the shares are sold.

A As your mother purchased the shares after September 1985 the price she paid for the shares will be your cost base when you sell them. You will pay tax on those shares only when they are sold and not beforehand. You could obtain some tax benefit if your mother sold enough shares each year so that the capital gain would not result in any tax being payable by her.

Borrowing

Q I currently live in an apartment I own outright. I want to upgrade, but would need to take out a loan to do so. I plan to keep my existing apartment and rent it out. Is it possible to take out the loan on my current apartment, so I can claim the interest as a tax deduction? I hear that this can be tricky from a tax perspective.

A The tax deductibility of interest is determined by how the funds are used, not what property is offered for security. In your situation you could only claim the interest on the amount of the loan related to when you purchased your apartment. The balance relating to the purchase of your new home would not be tax deductible.

You should consider selling your current apartment and making a tax-free gain. All the funds produced from the sale could be used to buy the new apartment you plan to live in. If your finances permit, you could then look for an investment property that would be paid for totally with a loan. Before deciding on either course of action, you should see a professional who provides tax planning investment advice.

Q I am currently purchasing a block of land that is due to settle around Christmas time. The plan is to commence building on it within a couple of months and building contracts are currently being organised. As this property is being purchased and built for rental and investment purposes, will the interest payable from the time of land settlement until occupancy be tax deductible by way of negative gearing?

A For many years it had been the ATO's view that interest paid during the construction phase was a capital cost. This view has now changed and, as long as there is a direct link between the loan and the investment property, and the length of time to commence construction is not excessive, the interest on the loan during construction will be deductible.

Depreciation of buildings

Q Instead of engaging a quantity surveyor to provide us with a depreciation schedule for our property, can we use the property purchase price as the 'original cost' then calculate 2.5 per cent depreciation based on that figure? What happens if the property was purchased five years ago and I have done my tax returns every year without claiming any depreciation on the property?

A You can't use your purchase cost to calculate the construction cost to claim the 2.5 per cent annual deduction.

The original cost of the property is made up of the value of the land, the value of the building, and the value of the fixtures and fitting in the property. The construction cost is an historical cost and, unless you can get this from the original owner or council records, you need to engage a quantity surveyor.

Under tax law most individuals can only amend two years of tax returns. Where a taxpayer has more complex tax issues, such as a property investor, they can amend up to four years of tax returns. The four-year time period is based on the assessment date for the year to be amended. For example, if your 2006 tax return was assessed on 31 July 2006 you would have until 31 July 2010 to request an amendment to include the depreciation claim missed.

Q If I sell my investment unit do I have to pay back all depreciation claimed previously?

A There are two types of depreciation. The first is the annual deduction for the reduction in value of fixtures and fittings, such as floor coverings and a stove, and the second is the 2.5 per cent building write off. When a property is sold, in most cases the fittings are considered to be sold at written-down value.

Where building costs have been claimed, and the property was purchased after 13 May 1997, the cost of the property must be decreased by the total amount of depreciation claimed. For example, if a property was purchased in 2001, for which the owners had claimed $10 000 in building write off, the cost used to calculate any capital gain would be decreased by $10 000.

Repairs or capital improvements?

Q For my investment property, what are the rules that differentiate maintenance costs and building costs. For instance, is repainting a property classed as maintenance or building? What is replacing an existing, but unsalvageable, paling fence?

A For a repair to be tax deductible it cannot improve the asset from the state it was in when you purchased it. If the fence was in a bad state of repair when you purchased the property, replacing it would not be a repair. If the fence was in good condition when you purchased the property, and has deteriorated since then, you could claim the cost of replacing it.

Q My partner and I have an investment property and the stove needs replacing. Can we deduct the cost of replacing the oven from our taxable income? The rest of the kitchen is also in a bad state, so could we claim any of the costs of replacing the kitchen?

A As you are planning to replace the entire stove, rather than repair it, the cost of the new stove will not be tax deductible. You will, however, be able to claim the written down value of the old stove in full and claim depreciation on the new one. Kitchen cupboards are not regarded as a depreciable item by the ATO. This means the cost of the new kitchen would be regarded as a structural improvement and you could claim the 2.5 per cent building write off.

Writing off capital items

Q I was hoping you could clarify depreciation on an investment property. I've just bought a new investment property that was recently renovated by the previous owners (new floorboards, kitchen bench tops, tiling and minor bathroom improvements). Are any of these features I can claim depreciation on? And could you clarify what else can be claimed? With this in mind, how do we calculate the value of depreciating assets?

A All of the items you mention are classed as structural improvements, and therefore can be depreciated at the 2.5 per cent depreciation rate. If the property was built after 1985, its original construction cost can also be written off at the same rate. In addition the cost of fixtures and fittings (such as curtains, light fittings, stoves and heaters) can be depreciated.

The safest way to arrive at the value for all of the depreciable items is to engage a quantity surveyor. This will cost approximately $500, but they will be able to assess the value of every depreciable item associated with the property and thus maximise your deduction. The only other way to do this is assess the current value by using the selling price of similar second-hand items offered for sale. You cannot value these items at replacement value.

Property purchase costs

Q I read your article about the tax myths for investment property — thanks for the information. I have just bought my first investment property, and settlement is due next month. Are the government charges and the solicitor fees I will be paying for this property tax deductible?

A As these costs are associated with the purchase of the property, and not with renting it, they will not be tax deductible against the rent but will form part of the cost of the property for capital gains tax. The exception to this will be any borrowing costs you pay. These can be written off over the term of the loan, or five years, whichever is the lesser.

Q For an investment property is the initial cleaning claimable as an expense and tax deductible?

A The costs associated with getting a property into a condition where it can be rented are not deductible, but form part of the purchase cost of the property.

Q I arranged for a buyer's agent to find me a property in Sydney and I eventually purchased one property through his company. Are any of the travel costs associated with my first visit, when I was getting a feel for the area that I was going to buy in, tax deductible? Is any of the buyer's agent's fee tax deductible?

A The cost of travel to look for a rental property is not tax deductible and does not form part of the purchase cost for capital gains tax. The fee charged by the buyer's agent will be part of the purchase cost of the property and used to decrease any future capital gain.

Resident or non-resident

Q I have a three-year contract in Doha, in Qatar. I rent an apartment there, but still have a house in Kiama, which my children live in. I receive no income from this. I pay no income tax on my wages in Doha and transfer money into my bank account to pay the mortgage in Australia. It is also an offset account for the loan that we pay bills out of. My accountant advised that I should be classified as a non-resident for Australian tax purposes as I have a three-year contract and rent an apartment in Doha. My wife has taken leave without pay and currently lives but does not work in Doha. Do you think I am a non-resident for tax purposes?

A The question of Australian tax residency can in some cases be very easy, while in others it can be extremely difficult. At the heart of deciding tax residency is the intention of the taxpayer. Where this cannot be established clearly, the ATO applies various tests to work out what a taxpayer's real intention is.

One of the tests used is to establish where the taxpayer normally resides. On its website the ATO gives the *Shorter Oxford Dictionary* definition of resides as, 'to dwell permanently, or for a considerable time, to have one's settled or usual abode, to live in or at a particular place'.

The ATO in deciding where someone normally resides takes account of where a person's family, business and employment ties are, and where they organise their financial affairs. Also taken into account is where their permanent place of abode is. In other words, where their residence is and where their family sleep at night.

In your case, as you have retained your home in Australia; you have not purchased a new home in Doha and are only renting; your wife has not resigned her employment but only taken leave without pay; you have a finite three-year contract that is not a permanent placement; and you maintain a bank account in Australia that you pay bills from; you would more than likely be classed as an Australian resident for tax purposes by the ATO.

Keeping tax records

Q I am in the process of culling some of my paperwork and I need to know how many previous years of tax paperwork I should keep.

A Where the documents relate to amounts claimed as tax deductions, such as rates and repairs for a rental property, they must be retained for five years from the date on the relevant notice of assessment. Paperwork relating to the purchase of an investment must be retained for five years after the notice of assessment that included the capital gain. Where a capital loss is involved, the five years would start from the date of the assessment that included the claim for the loss.

Subdividing property

Q I have a house with a big backyard and managed to get a permit to build a two-storey townhouse two years ago on the property. The construction has finished and I moved into my new townhouse last month. The construction loan was added to my old home loan. From a tax point of view what is my best option?

A To answer your questions it is first important to establish what you are trying to achieve. If you want to make your life as financially simple as possible, and reduce your non-investment debt to a minimum, it makes sense to subdivide the property now and sell off your old home.

By doing this now, the profit you make on the sale of your old home will be tax-free. The proceeds from this sale can then be used to pay off the debt on that home as well as the construction debt on the new unit. As the townhouse is your new principal place of residence, any profit you make when it is sold will also be tax free.

If you subdivided and rented your old home you would only get a tax deduction for the interest payable on the debt remaining on your original loan. This would mean instead of being negatively geared, you would produce a profit from your rental activities, which would be added to the rest of your income.

Q We have a principal place of residence that will be capital gains tax-free when we sell it. What are the CGT implications if I sell my backyard to a third party for development purposes?

A When a principal place of residence is subdivided, a taxpayer is left with two assets. The first is the land and the home on it that retain the CGT exemption. The second is the new piece of land created by the subdivision. If you sold a piece of your backyard, tax would be payable on the difference between the cost of that piece of land and the proceeds you receive.

CGT residence exemption

Q My girlfriend and I, along with another couple, purchased two semis, which were on the same land title back in 2007. My girlfriend and I live in one, and our friends the other. We have almost completed the legal process of subdividing them. No building changes have had to be made, as the houses and backyards have always been separate. Will we have to pay any capital gains tax when the subdivision occurs?

A In the first instance, as there is no change in beneficial ownership there should not be any tax payable. If, for some reason, the tax office wanted to rule that you were selling 50 per cent of your home to your friends, and they were selling 50 per cent of theirs to you, there should still not be any tax payable, because you would both be selling an interest in your main residence.

Q My wife and I have bought a two-hectare property on the outskirts of Sydney. The property has two homes on it, and our family will be living in one and we will most likely rent the other out. Are we able to negatively gear the second property? As soon as we rent it out, will we be up for CGT when we sell?

A You will be able to rent the second residence on the property and claim a tax deduction for its share of the costs such as rates, interest and land tax. It makes sense to have each residence and the land they stand on valued. To maximise your tax benefit you should consider having two loans for the property. One would be a residential loan for the value of the part of the property you will live in, less any cash you are contributing to the purchase, and the other an investment loan for the value of the rental property.

CGT will be payable on the rental property portion when you sell. The CGT exemption for a person's home is limited to land on up to two hectares. To decrease any potential capital gains tax bill you should, through fencing or in some other way, maximise the land attributable to your home.

Taxation of non-residents

Q I am an Australian working abroad for an international organisation and no longer pay taxes in Australia. I am interested in buying an investment property in Australia and wanted to know if there are any specific tax or legal considerations I should be aware of.

A From what you have said it would appear that you have sold your home in Australia and have a new home in the country where you are working. This will mean as a non-resident you only pay tax on Australian income.

If you purchase a rental property any profit you make will be taxed at 29 per cent up to $37 000 and then at the normal marginal rates from there. If you make a loss from the rental activities, this can be used to decrease any other income earned in Australia. If you still have a net rental loss, this is carried forward each year until other income is earned. If you sell the property and make a capital gain, tax will be payable on the gain.

Q I have been living and working with my family overseas since June 2005. We bought a home in Brisbane nine months before we departed and have rented it out the entire time we have been overseas. Rental property expenses have exceeded rental property income by about $12 000 per year for the past five years. How are these losses treated and is there a limit on the number of years we can claim tax losses and on the level of accumulated tax losses?

A If you return to Australia to live, the accumulated losses can be offset against income you earn from then on. There is no limit on the years or the amount of losses that can be carried forward. If you return to Australia after six years a portion of any gain you make when selling your former home will be taxable.

Q Does tax paid overseas on foreign income result in a refund in Australia; reduce tax payable on Australian income; or, if it exceeds the Australian tax payable, is the extra credit lost?

A Australian resident taxpayers can earn foreign income from a number of sources. It can come from income earned while working overseas; direct investments, such as shares in overseas companies; or Australian managed funds investing in overseas markets. In any of these cases tax can be deducted from the foreign income at its source.

An Australian resident taxpayer must declare all income they earn both here and overseas. Where tax has been deducted by the foreign country, this is included in the relevant section on your tax return. The amount of foreign tax paid reduces the Australian tax payable so that this income is not taxed twice.

Tax paid overseas can't produce a tax refund where it exceeds the Australian tax payable. The excess foreign tax credit can't be transferred and offset against other income, and it can't be carried forward to a later income year.

The cost of advice

Q I am a 65-year-old single male. Just before turning 65 I sought advice from a bank financial planner. Acting on his advice I combined my personal savings with my superannuation and started an allocated pension with a fund management business owned by the bank the adviser worked for. I selected the cash only investment option, and after fees I receive a 5.39 per cent return on the allocated pension. The upfront cost for this advice was $330 as a statement of advice fee, and I also paid a $2500 implementation fee.

The financial planner said that by implementing his advice I would be eligible for a part age pension as well as tax savings on the allocated pension. Now I wonder if I could have legally implemented all of this myself without going through a financial planner and saved myself $2830? In addition, could I have left the money in my normal bank account and term deposit and still have been eligible for a part age pension?

A   You have highlighted a major problem with the current financial advice industry that will be fixed from 1 July 2012 when commissions are banned. Your question also highlights the important principle of caveat emptor. When seeking financial advice the buyer should be truly aware.

The advice you got was sound, as your eligibility for the age pension did increase and tax has been saved. However, you could have avoided the implementation fee by starting a pension yourself with a super fund that has lower ongoing costs.

Instead of using a bank financial planner, who earns their money from commissions and sold you a bank product even though there are cheaper alternatives, it would have been better to get advice from a fee-for-service adviser who makes their money from the advice they give rather than from commissions or salary paid by the institution they work for. The advice might have cost more upfront, but you would have saved on the implementation fee and a more cost-effective super fund would have been recommended.

Superannuation or property

Q I am 32, earning around $105000 a year, plus the 9 per cent employer super, which is paid into my self managed superannuation fund (SMSF). My current super balance is $50000. My wife is currently not working, as we have two kids at home, and her super balance is $20000. I am planning to buy an investment property in my superannuation fund and would like to pay the maximum contributions allowed into my super account. Should I buy the investment property in superannuation or buy it outside super and negatively gear it?

A It would not make sense to buy the property in an SMSF given the level of borrowing needed. This is because an SMSF only pays tax at 15 per cent while you pay tax at 38.5 per cent. If you can afford the drain on cash flow it would be better to buy the property in your name, borrowing the maximum amount possible, as you would get the tax benefit of the negative gearing. The down side to this is that you would have to pay capital gains tax when you sell the property. I am surprised that you have an SMSF with only $50000 in it. Usually for an SMSF to be cost effective it should have a balance of at least $300000.

Tax treatment of a super pension

Q I commenced a transition to retirement pension in the 2008–09 financial year, and it is paid on 15 June every year. My date of birth is 7 November 1951. Will the pension received on 15 June 2012 be tax-free or will the amount be apportioned over the year?

A The tax treatment of superannuation is based on the age of the person when they receive the payment. As you will be over 60 when you receive your pension payment on 15 June 2012 it will be tax-free.

Transferring investments into super in an SMSF

Q My wife and I are the only trustees and members of our self managed superannuation fund (SMSF). We hold shares in our joint names outside the fund, and in the family trust company of which we are the only directors and beneficiaries. Will we have to pay capital gains tax if we do off-market transfers of these shares into our SMSF?

A When assets are transferred in specie to an SMSF there is still a change of ownership for capital gains tax purposes, so even though the shares are not being traded through the stock exchange and no brokerage fees are paid, capital gains tax can still be payable.

Q I am 62 and have $60 000 only in a newly set up SMSF. I work full-time and earn $70 000 a year. I own no property and have $300 000 in cash and shares. I obviously can't afford to retire for many years. I am considering salary sacrificing into super to save tax, but really need my salary to live on. What would be the implications of putting some of my assets into the SMSF? I am concerned that, if I do that, I won't be able to access money unless I retire.

A With the amount you currently have in your SMSF, if you don't increase the level of funds it has, your administration and compliance costs will be very high compared with an externally managed super fund. You should seriously consider transferring the shares and some of the cash into your SMSF. Before doing this you should check to see if this will result in a large capital gains tax bill on the transfer of your shares.

If your shares and cash did go into super you could draw a tax-free transition to retirement pension of about $15 000 a year. Based on your marginal tax rate, you could salary sacrifice $22 000 a year and be no worse off cash wise.

Taxation of super benefits

Q I am 62 years old, still working and hope to retire at 63. Can I take the full amount from my allocated pension without paying any tax?

A As you are aged over 60 the full amount of taxed superannuation benefits you receive will be tax-free.

Q I am 70 years old and recently sold my business. When I was self-employed I made tax-deductible contributions to a super fund. Now I want to withdraw my super funds and would like to know if the withdrawal will be taxable?

A As you are aged over 60, no tax will be payable on any amounts you withdraw. You should seriously consider leaving the superannuation in place and, instead of taking a lump sum, take pension payments. This is because you can receive a tax-free pension from your super while if you draw out all of your super you will pay income tax on income it earns. In addition, as you are over 65 you would need to meet the work test by working 40 hours in 30 consecutive days before being able to re-contribute the funds withdrawn.

Contribution rules for super after age 65

Q I am 59 years of age and understand that, after turning 65, I can contribute to super only if I 'pass the work test'. Does that mean I cannot work for more than 10 hours a week, or cannot work for more than 520 hours per year?

A To satisfy the work test you must work at least 40 hours over a continuous 30-day period in one financial year. This means the test is satisfied if you worked 40 hours in just one week, or worked 10 hours a week for four weeks. Once you have worked the 40 hours you do not have to work again in that financial year to be allowed to contribute super to a fund.

Q Are there any variations to the work test that would enable me to contribute to my super fund after I turn 65? It would appear to be limited to turning up at work for 40 hours over a 30-day period. How, for example, do self-employed people, such as barristers, many of whom continue to work beyond 65, pass the work test? I am pretty much retired, but do a bit of freelancing and consultancy work from time to time. Could this qualify, or do I have to 'get a job' for a month, which seems to me to be terribly artificial?

A The requirement for someone to work 40 hours in 30 continuous days is not limited to paid employment. It also extends to the self-employed. In your example, a barrister would meet the work test if they could show they had worked the required 40 hours. This proof could be in the form of time sheets kept or bills rendered to clients that detailed the hours worked.

With your freelancing you would need to keep some type of written record that shows the dates and times you worked. You would need to have billed for this time, as volunteer work does not qualify for the work test.

Q My wife and I have an industry super fund with $450 000 in it that pays an income stream. We also have two rental properties worth about $300 000 each. If we set up an SMSF and sell the two houses can we put the money from the sales, after paying the capital gains tax, into the SMSF and set up an income stream from it?

A Your ability to set up an SMSF, which could pay you an income stream, after contributing the net proceeds from the sale of the rental properties, depends on your age. If you are both under 65 you will be able to contribute up to $450 000 each as a non-concessional contribution from the sale proceeds. If you are aged 65 or older, you will both have to satisfy the work test and will then be able to contribute only up to $150 000 each.

You should seek advice from a tax planning professional. They could advise you whether you could reduce your capital gains tax payable by making tax-deductible self employed super contributions. This would be a benefit if the capital gain resulted in your paying tax at 30 per cent or more. A professional could also assess whether you should cease your current industry super fund income stream and roll the funds into your new SMSF.

Reducing tax on investment income

Q I am 57 years old and my wife is 54. I am employed full-time and paying a concessional rate of tax on my earnings. My wife works part-time and is on a similar rate of tax. We have $400000 invested in short-term deposits, earning between 6 and 7 per cent per year. This money is for our future retirement income. We would like to build this nest egg to $600000, then cut back on our work commitments, probably in two years time. I would like to know if there is a way of reducing or eliminating the tax on interest earned on these investments.

A The best place to have investments for retirement is in superannuation. This is because the income earned by the super fund will be, at worst, taxed at 15 per cent. You should consider contributing the $400000 as a non-concessional (after-tax) contribution for just yourself. As you are over 55 you could then commence a transition to retirement pension.

A super fund that pays a pension to a member pays no tax on any income earned on the investments used to fund the pension. As the pension you receive would be paid out of tax-free super benefits, it will not be included as taxable income by you. This would enable you to sacrifice some of your salary as extra super contributions.

A number of retirement and tax-planning options are available to you and your wife, including the type of super fund that will best suit you. You should seek advice from a fee-for-service professional who specialises in tax planning and superannuation.

Child support and a superannuation pension

Q I will soon be 60 and planning to retire. My income will be $50 000 a year in a tax-free pension from a self managed super fund. I currently pay child support and want to know if I will continue to be liable for child support when I retire. If the answer is 'yes', then what is the logic as I have already paid child support on the income that went into super?

A The amount of child support payable depends on the number of nights each parent has their children, the number of children, the age of the children and the income of each parent. Because the taxable income of an individual can be reduced by discretionary factors, such as negatively geared investments and amounts contributed to superannuation, various adjustments are made to each parent's taxable income to arrive at the income counted by Centrelink for liability for child support.

One area where adjustments are made is when a supporting parent retires and receives a superannuation pension. The child support system is all about ensuring children receive a proper level of child support from their parents, not what the parents would like to pay.

In arriving at the adjusted taxable income under the child support formula, some tax-free pensions and benefits are added to the taxable income of the relevant parent. Someone who is 60 or over and receives an income tax-free pension from a super fund could find that their taxable income could be adjusted for calculating child support depending on what percentage of the pension relates to taxable benefits.

Where the pension received is made up of taxable superannuation benefits the full amount of the pension is added back. Where the pension includes tax-free benefits, usually from non-concessional (after-tax) contributions, this part of the pension is not added back. In your case that means you will not pay extra child support on income contributed to a super fund that was previously counted for child support.

Eligibility for Centrelink benefits

Q We will be eligible for the age pension next year. Do we split the amount in our self managed super fund and apply the male and the female life expectancy to each, or do we apply the younger person's calculation? Also I have noticed Centrelink is now using the 2007 life expectancy tables. Does that life expectancy continue for the life of our super pension or does it change when new life expectancy tables are released in the future?

A Under Centrelink rules the total value of the combined superannuation for both of you is counted under the assets test. For the income test, the value of each member's account is counted. If a pension is not taken from the super fund, deeming rates are applied to each member's balance.

Where pensions are paid, the amount of income counted in the income test is the net value of the pension received, after deducting the purchase price of the pension. The purchase price is calculated at the time the pension commences using the life expectancy tables that apply at that date. This deductible purchase price does not change if new life expectancy tables are issued. Where the super pension paid is a reversionary pension (payable to a nominated beneficiary on the death of the pensioner), the age of the younger person is used to calculate the purchase price.

Q My father is aged 90 and receives a part age pension. My mother has recently passed away, leaving him her assets. He would like to know how much in assets he can have and how much earnings he can receive before his part pension will be affected.

A A single homeowning pensioner can have assets of up to $181750 without their pension being affected. Once a person exceeds this limit, their fortnightly pension is reduced by $1.50 for every $1000 of excess assets, and the pension ceases altogether when assets exceed $659250. A single non-homeowning pensioner can have assets of up to $313250 without the pension being affected; the pension cuts out once assets exceed $790750.

A single pensioner can earn up to $146 per fortnight in income without their pension being affected. Once this limit is exceeded the pension is reduced by 50 cents in the dollar. The age pension cuts out altogether once a single pensioner's income reaches $1578.20 per fortnight.

Q My grandmother is 75 years old and has been on a Centrelink pension since she came to Australia seven years ago. She has since saved up $25000 from her pension and wants to open a savings account so she can get interest. Will this affect the amount of Centrelink pension she is receiving?

A Under the pension income test, Centrelink deems an amount of income that has been earned on financial investments. Cash, whether it is in a cheque account, a term deposit or even a jam jar, has the deeming rules applied to it. A single person would need to have more than $96 355 in financial assets before the deeming rules affected the rate of pension they received. In your grandmother's case, she is well below this amount and her pension will not be affected by either the income test or the assets test.

Excess super contributions

Q I am a 47-year-old local government employee and for a few years now I have been contributing to my super via salary sacrifice. As I am under 50, I had to cut back last year to keep under the $25 000 limit on super contributions when the 9 per cent employer contribution was counted.

When I got my 2010 statement from the super fund, only 11 months had been credited as my employer was late sending the contribution for the last month of the year. I am concerned that this year, with 13 months' contributions, I will be over the limit and cop the extra tax, even though I have worked to keep my contributions to be just under the $25 000. How can I avoid being hit with the excess contributions tax?

A The situation you have outlined is not unique. Many Australians have been hit with excess contributions tax due to employers not paying superannuation contributions on time. A situation can even arise where an individual has two employers, and because they are both required to make the 9 per cent superannuation guarantee contribution, the member will have to pay the excess contributions tax and can do nothing about it.

For someone in your position, you will need to reduce your level of salary sacrifice contributions for the rest of the 2011 financial year so that the combined total of your super contributions will be below the $25 000 limit. This may not appear fair to you, due to your under-contribution for the 2010 year, but remember it is all about maximising tax revenue collections.

Accessing super

Q I am turning 60 in a few months, still working, earn about $30 000 from casual work, salary sacrifice $20 000 and have $200 000 in super. My husband is 70, has $110 000 in an account-based pension that pays $450 a month and he receives a Centrelink pension. We also receive dividends of around $1200 a year for me, and $420 for my husband. We still have a $20 000 mortgage. We would like to pay off our mortgage and fix the house. Can we withdraw $25 000 from either my husband's account-based pension or my superannuation later on when I turn 60 without affecting his Centrelink pension?

A As you are under 65 and still working you could not withdraw your superannuation unless you resigned from your current employer. It would be a better option for your husband to withdraw the $25 000 as a lump sum pension payment as he has access to this now. It would also be better for Centrelink purposes to do this, as your super is not counted as an asset until you reach age pension age.

Death and super

Q I understand no tax has to be paid if a super payment is made to a spouse on the death of a member. Does this extend to an ex-spouse of several years or, for that matter, a de facto partner?

A Two definitions of a dependant affect superannuation. The first is the definition used in superannuation law and the second is in income tax law. Both laws require there to have been an interdependency relationship between the fund member and the person receiving the payment.

Under superannuation law there is a relationship of interdependency when people have a close personal relationship and provide one or each other with financial support. The income tax law definition is tighter. It requires the financial support to be necessary and relied upon. This means that, under income tax law, if both your former spouse and de facto are financially dependent on you, they could qualify for the tax-free payment.

Self-employed super contributions

Q My wife is 45, has salary this income year of approximately $8000 and receives compulsory superannuation contributions from her employer. She is expecting a net capital gain of about $35 000 from the sale of a rental property. Is she eligible to contribute her after-tax income into her superannuation fund and claim this amount as a tax deduction? If she is eligible, what is the maximum amount she is able to contribute with her after-tax income and claim it as a deduction?

A As your wife has been employed this year, the 10 per cent income test will apply. Under this test a person is eligible to claim a tax deduction for a super contribution if their employment income is less than 10 per cent of their total assessable income. Unfortunately, the total income for your wife is $43 000 with her employment income being 19 per cent. This means she can't make a deductible contribution but she can make a non-concessional contribution.

GST and property

Q What are the GST consequences of someone building a new residential property to sell? Would your answer be different if the property in question was actually a main residence rather than an investment? Would the subsequent sale of the new dwelling attract GST in that case?

A A person or entity must register for GST if they are carrying on an enterprise and the expected GST taxable turnover will exceed $75 000. Carrying on an enterprise means something is done for the purpose of making a profit. In the tax office ruling setting out what constitutes carrying on an enterprise, the activity of subdividing land and building a dwelling to sell is classed as carrying on an enterprise.

As most properties would have a selling value of more than $75 000, the activity of subdividing a property, demolishing the existing residence, building two residences with one to be sold and the other one to be lived in, would be classed as carrying on an enterprise. If the existing home was not demolished and only one residence was built, which would become the owners' home, that is not carrying on an enterprise and the owners would not be liable for GST.

Where a person must register for GST they can claim all the GST they pay related to the residence they will be selling. They must also include GST in the selling price if it is sold within five years of its being completed. If the property is sold after five years, GST is not included in the selling price.

Q As an owner of a rental property do I need an ABN to be able to claim the GST that has been paid on any ongoing property expenses?

A In most cases people who own rental properties don't need to have an ABN. To be able to claim GST paid on expenses, a business must be registered for GST and be earning GST-taxable or GST-exempt income. Income received from domestic properties is classed as input-taxed income. Under this GST category, no GST is charged and no claim can be made for GST paid on expenses related to the earning of that income.

In your situation, if you are renting commercial properties this would be classed as GST-taxable income. If you are earning more than $75 000 a year you would need to be registered for GST and include GST in the rent you charge. You could then claim the GST you have paid on the expenses relating to that property.

If you only own residential property, there is no need to register for GST and there would be no point in registering. This is because residential rentals are classed as input taxed, and you could not claim the GST paid on the rental expenses.

Negative gearing

Q I recently bought my first investment property just before the end of the financial year. Unfortunately, I wasn't able to rent it out until early July, so can I negative gear anything for the last financial year, even though I received no income? Some of the things I was thinking of included interest, bank fees, body corporate charges, and an extra $2000 charge the body corporate imposed to repaint the whole building. It badly needed a new paint job, so I presume the repainting falls under maintenance.

A Although you received no income last year you will be able to claim a tax deduction for all the costs, except for the $2000 special levy. As the building was in need of a repaint when you purchased it, and the painting was not due to wear and tear related to rental activities, it would be regarded as an improvement. This cost will be added to the purchase cost of the unit and you should keep the body corporate invoice until five years after the unit is sold.

Appendix
Reference tables
and lists

Tax rates for individuals

Table 1: income tax rates for resident adults, 2010–11*

Annual taxable income ($)	Tax on income ($)		Tax rate on excess above lower threshold (%)
0–6000	0	plus	0
6001–37 000	0	plus	15
37 001–80 000	4 650	plus	30
80 001–180 000	17 550	plus	37
180 001 plus	54 550	plus	45

*Unless the 2011 federal budget changes these rates they are likely to apply for future years.

Table 2: after-tax earnings for resident adults, 2010–11

Annual income ($)	Annual tax payable ($)	Weekly income ($)	Weekly tax payable ($)	Annual after-tax income ($)	Weekly after-tax income ($)
10 000	0	192	0	10 000	192
15 000	0	288	0	15 000	288
20 000	600	385	12	19 400	373
25 000	1 350	481	26	23 650	455
30 000	2 100	577	40	27 900	537
35 000	2 850	673	55	32 150	618
40 000	5 550	769	107	34 450	663
45 000	7 050	865	136	37 950	730
50 000	8 550	962	164	41 450	797
55 000	10 050	1058	193	44 950	864
60 000	11 550	1154	222	48 450	932
65 000	13 050	1250	251	51 950	999
70 000	14 550	1346	280	55 450	1066
75 000	16 050	1442	309	58 950	1134
80 000	17 550	1538	338	62 450	1201
85 000	19 400	1635	373	65 600	1262
90 000	21 250	1731	409	68 750	1322
95 000	23 100	1827	444	71 900	1383
100 000	24 950	1923	480	75 050	1443
125 000	34 200	2404	658	90 800	1746
135 000	37 900	2596	729	97 100	1867
150 000	43 450	2885	836	106 550	2049
175 000	52 700	3365	1013	122 300	2352
180 000	54 550	3462	1049	125 450	2413
200 000	63 550	3846	1222	136 450	2624
225 000	74 800	4327	1438	150 200	2888
250 000	86 050	4808	1655	163 950	3153

*Tax payable is after allowing for low-income tax offsets.

Table 3: tax rates for non-resident adult individuals, 2010–11

Annual taxable income ($)	Tax on income ($)		Tax rate on excess above lower threshold (%)
0–37 000	0	plus	29
37 001–80 000	4 650	plus	30
80 001–180 000	17 550	plus	37
180 001 plus	54 550	plus	45

Table 4: tax rates for income of minors, 2010–11

Other income ($)	Tax rates
0–416	Nil
417–1307	Nil + 66% of the excess over $416
Over $1307	45% of the total amount of income that is not excepted income

Table 5: tax rates for deceased estates, 2010–11

Annual taxable income ($)	Tax on income ($)		Tax rate on excess above lower threshold (%)
Less than 3 years since death			
Nil–6000	0	plus	0
6001–37 000	4 650	plus	15
80 001–180 000	17 550	plus	37
180 001 plus	54 550	plus	45
3 years or more since death			
Nil–416	0	plus	0
417–594	0	plus	50
595–37 000	89	plus	15
37 001–80 000	5 550	plus	30
80 001–180 000	18 450	plus	37
180 001 plus	55 450	plus	45

Table 6: Medicare levy thresholds for individuals, 2009–10*

Category	Lower threshold ($)	Upper threshold $)
Individual eligible for the senior Australian tax offset	29 867	35 137
Individual eligible for the pensioner tax offset	27 697	32 584
All other taxpayers	18 488	21 750

*The 2010–11 thresholds will be announced in the 2011 federal budget.

Table 7: Medicare levy surcharge thresholds for taxpayers with children, 2009–10*

Number of dependent children or students	Singles ($)	Family ($)
0	73 000	146 000
1	146 000	146 000
2	147 500	147 500
3	149 000	149 000
4	150 500	150 500
5	152 000	152 000
Each extra child	Add 1500	Add 1500

*The 2010–11 thresholds will be announced in the 2011 federal budget.

Table 8: HELP and HECS repayment thresholds and rates, 2010–11

HELP repayment income (HRI) ($)	Repayment rate as a percentage of HRI
Below 44 912	Nil
44 912–50 028	4.0
50 029–55 143	4.5
55 144–58 041	5.0
58 042–62 390	5.5
62 391–67 570	6.0
67 571–71 126	6.5

HELP repayment income (HRI) ($)	Repayment rate as a percentage of HRI
71 127–78 273	7.0
78 274–83 407	7.5
83 408 plus	8.0

Tax offsets

Table 9: low-income tax offset, 2010–11

Income ($)	Offset ($)
7 500	1500
10 000	1500
15 000	1500
20 000	1500
25 000	1500
30 000	1500
32 500	1400
35 000	1300
37 500	1200
40 000	1100
42 500	1000
45 000	900
47 500	800
50 000	700
52 500	600
55 000	500
57 500	400
60 000	300
62 500	200
65 000	100
67 500	0

Table 10: senior Australian tax offset, 2010–11

	Maximum offset* ($)	Shadeout threshold ($)	Income at which offset cuts out ($)
Single	2230	30685	48525
Couple (each)	1602	26680	39496
Couple separated due to illness (each)	2040	29600	45920

*Rebate reduces by 12.5c for each $1 of taxable income above the shadeout threshold.

Table 11: other tax offsets

Description	Amount of offset	Income threshold ($)	Cut-off threshold ($)
Dependent spouse	$2286	282	9426
Mature age worker	5% of income	0	10000
Mature age worker	$500	10000	63000
Superannuation pension tax offset	15%		
Medical expenses over $2000	20%		

Table 12: maximum concessional super contributions, 2009–13

Age person turns during the 2010–11 tax year	2009–10 ($)	2010–11 ($)	2011–12 ($)	2012–13 ($)
50 and over	50000	50000	50000	25000
49	25000	50000	50000	25000
48	25000	25000	25000	25000
47 and younger	25000	25000	25000	25000

Table 13: minimum superannuation pension rates, ages 55–95+

Age of super fund member	Minimum pension rate (%)
55–64	4
65–74	5
75–79	6
80–84	7
85–89	9
90–94	11
95 and over	14

Table 14: age when you can access your super

Age	Conditions
65 and over	No conditions—super can be accessed at any time
60–64	Termination of current employment
	Through a transition to retirement pension
55–59	Retires and not intending to work more than 10 hours a week
	Severe financial hardship
	Terminal illness
	Compassionate grounds
	Permanent incapacity
	Temporary incapacity
	Death
18–65	Departing Australia permanently
All ages	Death or to pay excess contributions tax

Table 15: taxation of lump sum super payments

Age of person receiving payment	Tax rate payable
60 and over	Nil
55–59	
Up to tax-free threshold – $160 000 for 2010–11	Nil
Excess over tax-free threshold	15%
54 and younger	20%
Permanent invalidity payments	Nil
Temporary invalidity payments	At marginal tax rate
Death benefits	
To dependants	Nil
To non-dependants — taxed benefits	15%
— untaxed benefits	30%

Table 16: tax payable on superannuation pensions

Age of person receiving pension	Tax rate payable
60 and over	Nil
55–59	At marginal rate less 15% super pension rebate
54 and younger	At marginal tax rate
Permanent invalidity payments	Nil
Temporary invalidity payments	At marginal tax rate
Death benefits	
To dependants over 60	Nil
To dependants under 60	At marginal rate less 15% super pension rebate

Table 17: eligibility for base rate of Family Tax Benefit Part A, 1 January 2011

No. of children 0–12 years	Actual annual family income limit beyond which only base rate is paid ($)*			
	No. of children 13–15 years			
	Nil	1	2	3
Nil		65 609	86 104	106 599
1	59 331	79 826	100 321	120 815
2	73 548	94 043	114 537	135 032
3	87 765	108 259	128 754	149 249

*Income limit will be higher if individual is eligible for rent assistance.

Table 18: income limit where eligibility for Family Tax Benefit Part A stops, 1 January 2011

No. of children 0–17 years	Actual annual family income limit at which Family Tax Benefit A stops ($)			
	No. of children 18–24 years			
	Nil	1	2	3
Nil		100 290	110 060	120 791
1	98 769	108 539	119 270	130 001
2	107 018	117 749	128 480	139 211
3	116 229	126 960	137 691	148 422

*These figures do not include the family tax benefit supplement that is paid annually.

Table 19: eligibility for Family Tax Benefit Part B, 1 January 2011

Income earned by	Benefit cuts out when income exceeds ($)
Primary income earner	150 000
Secondary income earner*	
Youngest child under 5	24 291
Youngest child aged 5–18	18 907

*The secondary income earner can earn up to $4745 each year before it affects the rate of Family Tax Benefit Part B. Payments are reduced by 20 cents for each dollar of income earned over $4745.

Table 20: assets test limits for allowances and full pensions, 1 January 2011*

Family situation	For allowances and full pension assets must be less than† ($)	
	For homeowners	For non-homeowners
Single	181750	313250
Couple (combined)	258000	389500
Couple separated by illness (couple combined)	258000	389500
One partner eligible (combined assets)	258000	389500

*These limits change twice yearly in March and September.

†Once the assets test limit is exceeded, the full pension decreases by $1.50 per fortnight for every $1000 in excess.

Table 21: assets test limits for part pensions, 1 January 2011*

Family situation	For part pension assets must be less than ($)	
	For homeowners	For non-homeowners
Single	659250	790750
Couple (combined)	978000	1109500
Couple separated by illness (couple combined)	1213000	1344500
One partner eligible (combined assets)	978000	1109500

Transitional homeowner

Family situation	For homeowners	For non-homeowners
Single	611000	742500
Couple (combined)	951500	1083000
Couple separated by illness (couple combined)	1116500	1248000
One partner eligible (combined assets)	951500	1083000

*These limits change twice yearly in March and September.

Table 22: income test for pensions, 1 January 2011*

Family situation	Lower threshold† ($) For full pension/ allowance (per fortnight)	Upper threshold ($) For part pension (per fortnight)
Single	Up to 146	Less than 1578.20
Couple (combined)	Up to 256	Less than 2415.20
Couple separated by illness (couple combined)	Up to 256	Less than 3120.40

*These limits change twice yearly in March and September.

†Once the lower threshold is exceeded, the fortnightly pension decreases by 50 cents for each $1 earned until the upper threshold is reached. Due to pension rates changing, the thresholds shown also change. There are also transitional income thresholds that apply to people who were on the pension before the recent changes that work differently. The Centrelink website <www.centrelink.gov.au> will have the latest information, and their A to Z index makes it easy to find the information you need.

Table 23: life expectancy table for pensions that commenced on or after 1 January 2010

Age	M	F	Age	M	F	Age	M	F
50	31.43	35.17	70	14.76	17.42	90	4.36	4.91
51	30.53	34.24	71	14.04	16.61	91	4.11	4.57
52	29.63	33.31	72	13.33	15.82	92	3.89	4.27
53	28.73	32.38	73	12.64	15.03	93	3.69	3.99
54	27.84	31.45	74	11.96	14.27	94	3.51	3.75
55	26.95	30.53	75	11.31	13.51	95	3.36	3.53
56	26.08	29.61	76	10.68	12.78	96	3.22	3.33
57	25.20	28.70	77	10.07	12.05	97	3.10	3.16
58	24.34	27.79	78	9.48	11.35	98	2.99	3.00
59	23.48	26.89	79	8.92	10.67	99	2.90	2.86
60	22.63	26.00	80	8.38	10.01	100	2.81	2.74
61	21.79	25.11	81	7.86	9.37	101	2.73	2.63
62	20.96	24.23	82	7.36	8.75	102	2.66	2.54
63	20.14	23.35	83	6.89	8.17	103	2.60	2.46

Table 23 *(cont'd)*: life expectancy table for pensions that commenced on or after 1 January 2010

Age	M	F	Age	M	F	Age	M	F
64	19.34	22.48	84	6.45	7.61	104	2.54	2.38
65	18.54	21.62	85	6.03	7.08	105	2.49	2.32
66	17.76	20.76	86	5.64	6.58	106	2.44	2.26
67	16.99	19.92	87	5.27	6.11	107	2.40	2.20
68	16.24	19.08	88	4.94	5.68	108	2.35	2.15
69	15.49	18.24	89	4.63	5.28	109	2.30	2.09

Glossary

Account-based pension A pension paid from a super fund when someone has reached retirement age. These pensions are extremely flexible and tend to be paid in monthly instalments. Depending on the person's age, a minimum pension must be taken each year, but no maximum is set. These pensions are extremely popular as they allow members to withdraw lump sums as well as a regular pension.

Accumulation fund A superannuation fund where all of the member's benefits are a combination of contributions made and income earned, minus administration costs deducted and taxes paid.

Accumulation phase The stage before retirement when people are building up their retirement assets and their superannuation.

Adjusted fringe benefits The amount shown on a person's PAYG annual summary for reportable fringe benefits multiplied by 53.5 per cent.

Adjusted taxable income A figure used by the ATO when assessing an individual's eligibility for tax offsets. It is calculated by taking a person's taxable income and adding to it adjusted fringe benefits, tax-free pensions or benefits, target foreign income, reportable super contributions and total net investment losses. This figure is reduced by deductible child maintenance expenditure.

Allocated pension (AP) A pension paid from a superannuation fund before the simplified superannuation system was introduced. It was replaced by the account-based pension.

APRA *see* Australian Prudential Regulation Authority

Arms length transaction A transaction between two related or connected parties conducted as if they were unrelated, so that there is no question of a conflict of interest.

Assessable income The income on which a person or entity pays tax. It includes income from employment, company dividends, interest earned, distributions from trusts and partnerships, business profit, rental income, taxable capital gains, foreign income and any other income that has to be shown on a tax return.

Asset allocation The division of a person's investments over the different asset classes. Asset allocation is often based on a person's stage in life or their tolerance to risk.

Asset classes The different types of investments. They include cash, shares, property, fixed interest and alternatives.

ATO *see* Australian Taxation Office

Australian Prudential Regulation Authority (APRA) The body established in 1998 to regulate and control the financial services industry. The types of businesses regulated by APRA include banks, credit unions, building societies, general insurance and reinsurance companies, life insurance, friendly societies and most super funds. Super funds not regulated by APRA are self managed super funds, which are controlled by the ATO.

Australian Taxation Office (ATO) The body set up to administer the various federal taxes, including income tax, capital gains tax, and the goods and services tax. It is also responsible for regulation and control of self managed super funds, and the administration of legislation relating to the superannuation guarantee and super choice.

Average weekly ordinary times earnings (AWOTE) The average of full-time adult weekly ordinary time earnings for all persons in Australia. It excludes overtime earned. The increase in this average is a benchmark used when various government thresholds are increased over time, including those related to superannuation.

Benefits phase   The phase in a super fund when a member retires and commences taking super benefits in the form of a pension. It is sometimes referred to as the drawdown phase.

Bona fide redundancy payments   Payments by an employer to an employee who has been made redundant. For a person to be classified as redundant, the position they previously worked in cannot be given to another employee.

Capital gains tax (CGT)   The tax payable when an asset (such as property, shares, collectibles or investments) is sold for a profit. It is applied to assets purchased since 19 September 1985.

Capital gains tax exempt   You do not have to pay CGT on the sale of some assets. These include assets purchased before 19 September 1985, a person's home and cars, and active assets available for the small business retirement exemption.

Commercial funds   Super funds run by insurance companies and financial institutions for a profit.

Commutation   The conversion of an account-based pension into a lump sum that is either paid out or rolled back into a super fund in the accumulation phase.

Complying superannuation fund   A super fund that meets all of the relevant government standards set out in the *Superannuation (Industry) Supervision Act* (*SIS Act*) *1993* and has elected to be regulated under the act. A complying superannuation fund is eligible for concessional tax treatment.

Compound interest   When interest earned on an investment is not taken as cash but is added to the original investment, the value of the investment increases and interest is then earned on the original amount invested and the interest accumulated.

Concessional component   The part of payments from either super funds or employers that are made up of redundancy payments, invalidity payments and payments from approved early retirement schemes paid before 1 July 1994.

Concessional contributions   Super contributions that are made by employers or self-employed people, including salary sacrifice super contributions. A tax benefit is obtained when these contributions are made. This tax benefit depends on who makes the contributions but varies from zero to 30 per cent for individuals, and 15 per cent for companies. The tax benefit is the difference between the tax rate paid by the person or entity making the contribution and the 15 per cent tax paid by a super fund. Also described as before-tax contributions and deductible contributions.

Concessional tax treatment   Complying super funds receive benefits that result in tax being paid at 15 per cent on all contributions and income, and 10 per cent on any qualifying capital gains. In addition, when funds are in pension phase no tax is paid on earnings.

Condition of release   The conditions laid down by law that enable a trustee of a super fund to pay out benefits to members. The conditions of release are met depending on a person's age, employment status and other circumstances specified in the *Superannuation (Industry) Supervision Act (SIS Act) 1993.*

Contributions phase   The initial phase in a super fund goes through when it receives employer or member contributions.

Deductible child maintenance expenditure   The amount of child support a parent pays to another person to maintain the parent's natural or adopted children following separation.

Deductible contributions   *see* Concessional contributions

Default option   The super fund or investment choice that a person is allocated to when they do not choose where they want their super contributions to go.

Defined benefit fund   A superannuation fund where a member's final benefit is dependent on a stated or defined benefit calculation.

This could be a multiple of the member's final average salary. These funds tend to be provided by large companies and government organisations, and do not apply to SMSFs.

Dividend yield The value of the dividends paid per share, or expected to be paid, by a company, divided by the price of the share. This produces an investment return rate investors should earn as an income that does not include any expected capital growth.

Early retirement schemes Schemes often used by employers when they want to decrease their workforce. Under such schemes all employees are offered the chance to resign and retire.

Eligible termination payment (ETP) A payment from an employer or a super fund to an employee upon retirement, resignation, retrenchment or disablement. It can be taken as a lump sum payment, or in some cases can be rolled over into a super fund.

Entity Any type of taxation structure. It includes companies, unit trusts, discretionary or family trusts, super funds, partnerships and individuals.

Franking credits The tax paid by Australian companies for which a shareholder gets a tax credit of 30 per cent. This credit reduces the tax payable on dividends received and can result in a tax refund.

Fringe benefits tax (FBT) A system brought in to tax benefits taken by employees in forms other than salaries or wages.

General interest charge (GIC) The penalty levied by the tax office in the form of interest when tax has been underpaid.

Hedging A financial term for limiting the risk in certain circumstances. When it comes to shares and foreign currency, hedging can take the form of forward contracts. Forward contracts are basically a commitment to buy or sell something at a predetermined price at a future date.

Income tax The tax paid on the net taxable income earned by individuals, companies, super funds and other entities.

Incurred An accounting term that relates to when a liability comes into existence. Most individual investors account for income and costs on a cash basis: this means income is not assessable until it is received and costs are not deductible until they are paid. Businesses, however, often use the accrual method of accounting. This means income is assessable when it is earned and costs are deductible when they are incurred.

Industry and union funds Before the introduction of the superannuation guarantee system by the Hawke Labor government super funds tended to be provided by commercial institutions. Since then, unions and industry groups have set up industry funds where the aim is not to make a profit but to provide benefits to members. Industry funds often cover a specific industry or a range of industries.

In-house asset An asset of a super fund that is a loan to, or an investment in, a related party of the fund; an investment in a related trust of the fund; or an asset of the fund subject to a lease or lease arrangement between a trustee of the fund and a related party of the fund.

Invalidity payment A payment by either a super fund or an employer when a person ceases employment as a result of partial or total disablement. It can be paid as either a lump sum or an income stream, such as a pension.

Investment phase The phase in a super fund before the pension phase. During this phase the fund receives contributions and income from the investments made.

Listed property trust (LPT) A unit trust listed on a stock exchange that earns income from property ownership and other activities.

Low income tax offset (LOTI) A tax offset that reduces income tax payable by individuals depending on their total taxable income.

Lump sum benefit super fund A super fund that can either make lump sum payments to members or pay them a pension.

Managed fund A form of unit trust that pools many investors' money and buys investments in the chosen investment sector, such as shares, fixed interest and property.

Management expense ratio (MER) A measure of the total ongoing fees that investors in a managed fund pay annually. It generally includes the management fee, in addition to other expenses, such as custodian fees, adviser trail brokerage and fund auditing expenses. It is calculated by dividing the total expenses of the fund by the number of investment units on issue, and it is expressed as an annual percentage figure.

Margin lending scheme A method of finance often linked with investing in shares. The shares purchased under a margin lending facility are used as security for the loan. Where the value of the shares used for security drops below a pre-set percentage of the amount borrowed, the investor must either contribute more cash or sell shares to reduce the amount borrowed.

Market-linked pension A pension introduced under the Howard government that could be paid by self managed super funds as a complying or lifetime pension.

Medicare levy A charge levied by the federal government on individuals who have net taxable income above a set level. The level changes each year and differs between single taxpayers and married taxpayers. The Medicare levy rate is 1.5 per cent of a person's taxable income.

Medicare levy surcharge Where individuals and couples do not have private health insurance, and their income exceeds a pre-set level, which for the 2010–11 year is $77000 for individuals and $154000 for couples, a Medicare levy surcharge of 1 per cent is paid on their taxable income.

Net capital gain The amount of a capital gain made on the sale of an asset that must be included in assessable income. It is the gain remaining after deducting any applicable concessions, such as the 50 per cent general concession, where the investment has been held for more than 12 months, or any of the small business CGT concessions. In a super fund, one-third of the gain is deducted, resulting in super funds paying 10 per cent tax on an eligible capital gain.

Net tangible asset backing (NTA) The total value of a listed company's assets, excluding intangible assets, such as goodwill and patents, less the total of the company's liabilities. This amount is divided by the total number of listed shares for the company to arrive at an NTA value per share.

Non-commutable pension A pension, such as a transition to retirement (TTR) pension that cannot be converted into a lump sum payment. A non-commutable pension can, however, be rolled back into a super fund account in the accumulation phase.

Non-complying superannuation fund A super fund that does not meet all the operational regulations laid down by APRA and the ATO. These super funds pay tax on all contributions, income and accumulated benefits at the top marginal tax rate.

Non-concessional contributions Contributions to a super fund for which no tax deduction has been allowed; in other words, super contributions made from after-tax money.

Novated lease A form of car finance used when a person packages their salary so that their employer provides them with a car for their personal use. Novated leases are taken out in the name of the employee, who owns the car, but the employer is shown as responsible for making the lease payments out of the employee's pre-tax salary.

Pay as you go (PAYG) The system that was created when GST was introduced in 2000. It requires employers to deduct tax from employees' pay, called PAYG Withholding, and requires the self-employed and investors to pay tax over the course of a year, which is called the PAYG Instalment system.

Pension phase Once a super fund account commences paying a pension it ceases to be in accumulation phase. The pension paid could be a transition to retirement (TTR) pension or an account-based pension. Super fund accounts in pension phase pay no income tax. Members have the ability to split their super balance into components so that part of their fund can be in pension phase, while the other part is in accumulation phase.

Post-June 1994 invalidity payments The portion of an ETP paid to a person when they ceased employment as a result of their not being able to be employed ever again in a capacity for which they are reasonably qualified by education, training or experience.

Pre-1983 superannuation The superannuation relating to a member's service before 1 July 1983. This component was calculated by dividing the value of the member's super by the total number of days they had worked, and multiplying that by the number of days worked before 1 July 1983. After 1 July 2007 pre-1983 superannuation became one of the components of tax-free super benefits.

Preservation age The age at which a super fund member can access their super, provided they meet a condition of release, such as retirement.

Preserved benefits A super fund member's benefits that they cannot access because they have not reached preservation age, or met any other conditions of release.

Regulated superannuation fund A super fund that meets all of the regulations laid down by the *Superannuation (Industry) Supervision Act (SIS Act) 1993*. As such, they receive all the tax benefits of a complying super fund.

Related party An individual or entity that is related to an entity or member of a super fund. This can include family members or entities that a family member or relative has an ownership in.

Reportable super contributions The super contributions that an employer must include on an individual's PAYG summary certificate, showing the value of super contributions made as a result of a salary sacrifice arrangement. These contributions are now counted in some tests when assessing a person's eligibility for tax and other concessions.

Retirement age   The age at which people can access super. For anyone born before 1 July 1960 it is age 55, and it increases to 60 for people born after 30 June 1964.

Retirement exemption   A tax exemption available to qualifying taxpayers for capital gains made on the sale of active business assets.

Reversionary beneficiary   The person who receives a pension upon the death of the original pensioner as a result of being the pensioner's nominated beneficiary.

Reversionary pension   A pension that is payable to a nominated beneficiary upon the death of the original member.

Rollover   The process by which a super fund member transfers their superannuation or an employer ETP, usually before retirement, into a super fund, approved deposit fund or deferred annuity.

Salary sacrifice   In addition to the 9 per cent super contribution by employers, employees can give up, or sacrifice, part of their salary or wage and have it contributed to their super fund as an extra contribution. By doing this, they make extra super contributions taxed at 15 per cent, which had they received the money as a salary or wage they would have paid tax at between 16.5 per cent and 46.5 per cent (including Medicare levy).

Self-employed   Someone who does not have any super contributions made on their behalf by an employer, or receives only minor employer super contributions.

Self managed super fund (SMSF)   A super fund that is regulated by the ATO and has no more than four members, who are also the trustees of the fund.

Separately managed account (SMA)   A way of investing in the sharemarket where a share specialist buys shares on behalf of the investor; the ownership of the shares is in the investor's name.

Special income   Income diverted into an SMSF to avoid tax. As such it is taxed at the top marginal tax rate in the super fund.

Superannuation benefits   A member's benefits in a super fund.

Superannuation choice   A system introduced under the Howard Liberal government designed to create more choice and flexibility for super fund members.

Superannuation guarantee charge (SGC)   A penalty imposed by the ATO when an employer fails to make a super contribution on behalf of an employee.

Superannuation guarantee system (SGS)   The system requiring employers to contribute 9 per cent of an employee's salary as superannuation. Employees must earn more than $450 in a month to be eligible for super guarantee payments.

Superannuation Industry (Supervision) Act (SIS Act) 1993   The Commonwealth legislation that sets out the rules and regulations that govern the activities of super funds approved deposit funds and other retirement funds and entitles them to receive concessional tax treatment.

Target foreign income   Income that is earned overseas and not included in your assessable income because it is exempt from Australian tax. It includes regular receipts of money and gifts received from relatives living overseas, business and investment income from overseas, and foreign source income earned while you were a temporary resident.

Tax file number (TFN)   The unique number issued to taxpayers to identify them by the Australian Tax Office.

Tax offset   Tax concessions that reduce the amount of tax payable by an individual. They are not tax deductions, which decrease taxable income; they are reductions in the final tax paid by an individual.

Tax rebate   *see* Tax offset

Taxable superannuation benefits A member's benefits in a super fund that are taxable if taken before they reach 60; they include concessional (tax-deductible) contributions and accumulated income.

Term allocated pension A complying whole-of-life pension. Also known as a market-linked pension.

Total income The term used when assessing a person's eligibility for the government co-contribution scheme. It includes all assessable income, including employment and investment income, plus the total of any reportable fringe benefits and super benefits a person received during the year in which a co-contributions is sought.

Trail commissions Commissions charged by advisers as an annual percentage of the funds in a super fund or managed investment. They can range from as low as 0.11 per cent up to and more than 1.5 per cent. As they are a regular fee, deducted up to monthly by the super fund or managed fund; members of a fund may not be aware of the deduction of these costs.

Transition to retirement pension (TTR) A pension paid by a superannuation fund to members in the form of a non-commutable pension once they reach retirement age. People do not have to resign from their employer to be eligible for a TTR.

Trustee An individual or company that acts as trustee for a trust, such as a super fund, unit trust or family discretionary trust. Trustee are responsible for the day-to-day running of a trust, and in the case of a super fund, also ensuring that all of the relevant regulations are met.

Undeducted contributions The former name of non-concessional contributions. Also known as after-tax contributions.

Untaxed scheme A super fund that does not pay tax on contributions or earnings. These schemes are usually run by governments and public service organisations, such as the police, for the benefit of their employees.

Whole-of-life pension A super pension paid until a member dies.

Wholesale managed funds Managed funds that require a minimum amount to be invested; they are not offered to the general public. Just as it is with other wholesale products, such as fruit, where the purchaser must buy in bulk, the cost is cheaper than if a retail product had been purchased. For managed funds this comes in the form of lower fees charged by the fund manager.

Wrap account An account that allows investors to invest in wholesale managed funds regardless of the amount being invested. Wrap accounts also make it easier for a person to invest in a large number of different managed funds through the administration and accounting services provided by wrap account providers. This means an investor has to complete only one application form and provide only one cheque, even though they may be investing with 10 different fund managers.

The provider of the wrap account charges the investor an administration fee as a percentage of the total funds invested. Because retail managed funds have higher management fees, the actual cost of a wrap account to the investor, taking into account the wholesale manager's fees and the wrap administration fee, can in many cases be about the same.

Unfortunately for many investors, financial advisers have used wrap accounts as a source of revenue by adding a trail commission, which is paid to them on top of the fee charged by the wrap administrator. Investors who do not pay this trail commission, but pay an agreed fee to their adviser for ongoing advice or if they want to look after their own ongoing investments affairs and pay no fee, end up with an investment management service that makes it easier for them to invest and keep track of their investments at not much if anything more than had they invested in the retail version of the managed fund.

Index

taxation, *see also* income tax;
deductions; capital gains tax;
goods and services tax; offsets and
rebates, tax; superannuation
—rates 265–267
—records 244
—residency 75–76, 128–129,
242–243, 247–248
testamentary trust 166
total and permanent disability (TPD)
insurance 159–160
transition to retirement pension 32,
34, 35, 144–146, 252
—combined with contributions,
145, 146

trauma insurance 160–161
trusts, *see* family discretionary
trust; testamentary trust; unit
trusts

unit trusts 97, 101–102, 112
unrestricted non-preserved benefits
39, 40

wills, *see* estate planning
work bonus 53
working past pension age 53–55
work test 33, 35, 149, 253–254